ABOVE THE LINE

ABOVE
THE
LINE

ABOVE THE LINE

HOW TO CREATE A COMPANY CULTURE THAT ENGAGES EMPLOYEES,
DELIGHTS CUSTOMERS AND DELIVERS RESULTS

MICHAEL HENDERSON
THE CORPORATE ANTHROPOLOGIST

WILEY

First published in 2014 by John Wiley & Sons Australia, Ltd
42 McDougall St, Milton Qld 4064

Office also in Melbourne

Typeset in 12/14.5 pt Bembo Std

© Above 200 Limited 2014

The moral rights of the author have been asserted

National Library of Australia Cataloguing-in-Publication data:

Author:	Henderson, Michael
Title:	Above the Line: How to Create a Company Culture that Engages Employees, Delights Customers and Delivers Results / Michael Henderson.
ISBN:	9780730312505 (pbk)
	9780730312512 (ebook)
Notes:	Includes index.
Subjects:	Corporate culture.
	Corporations — Sociological aspects.
	Organisational behaviour.
	Customer services.
	Customer relations.
	Industrial relations.
Dewey Number:	302.35

Cover design by Xou Creative

Printed in Singapore by C.O.S. Printers Pte Ltd

10 9 8 7 6 5 4 3 2 1

Disclaimer
The material in this publication is of the nature of general comment only, and neither purports nor intends to be advice. Readers should not act on the basis of any matter in this publication without considering (and if appropriate, taking) professional advice with due regard to their own particular circumstances. The author and publisher expressly disclaim all and any liability to any person, whether a purchaser of this publication or not, in respect of anything and of the consequences of anything done or omitted to be done by any such person in reliance, whether whole or partial, upon the whole or any part of the contents of this publication.

Everything should be made as simple as possible, but not simpler.

Albert Einstein

Dedicated to Shar Henderson

Contents

Part IV: Culture planning 197

About the author

Source: © Tom Roberton

Michael Henderson has had a lifelong passion for culture. Born in the United Kingdom, raised in Africa and now living in New Zealand, he has the advantage of being able to quickly understand the essence of a culture, including the values and underlying assumptions, and explain it to others. He is one of the few people working in business today who can teach organisations how to see, understand and transform culture in real terms.

Michael graduated from Auckland University in 1985 with a Bachelor of Arts degree, majoring in anthropology. He then built on this academic knowledge by travelling extensively over the next seven years, reviewing more than 70 cultures and tribes across 40 countries.

For the past 16 years Michael has applied his unique combination of anthropological skills and practical business experience to support his clients in a variety of ways to unlock the power of cultures within their organisations.

He is the best-selling author of five books on the impact and benefits of mastering company culture and human values.

Michael has been awarded the Thought Leader Mentor of the Year award by Thought Leaders Global Ltd in recognition of his innovative and ground-breaking approaches to helping his clients develop and grow their business. Michael is a partner at Thought Leaders Global and their Anthropologist in Residence.

Acknowledgements

Having already written several books on organisational culture, I had to ask myself, 'Does the world really need another?' Writing a book requires no small amount of effort from both the author and the publishing team, comprising the commissioning editor, the editor, design and layout artist, sales and marketing team, and the cover design artist. As an author, before you even begin to think about putting pen to paper, or finger tips to keyboards, you have to consider if you genuinely have anything worthwhile to say or share, before you ask all these people to become engaged and support your effort with all their combined experience, talents, insights and advice.

So, first, my clients deserve a huge amount of appreciation and thanks for allowing me to share my ideas with them and then for having the commitment and perseverance to apply the ideas in their organisations. This interest and take-up by clients is the best motivation an author could have as it clearly indicates the ideas are worthy and had been tested in the most demanding environment the fast-changing, cynical world of business. Ineffective ideas don't last long when people, time, money, energy, profits, customers and shareholders are at stake.

Second, I wish to thank professional editor Meryl Potter who had the thankless task of translating the ideas in my original manuscript into written English. Unfortunately I think faster than I can type, and so my brain is often a sentence or paragraph ahead of my typing fingers. This resulted in regular doses of chaos appearing in the pages of the first draft. Meryl bravely ventured into my written jungle and, with editing machete and torch in hand, slashed the unnecessary away and illuminated the bits worth highlighting. This book is at least twice if not three times better than the original draft due to Meryl's input. If you enjoy this book and learn from it you probably have Meryl to thank for it.

I also wish to thank the team at Wiley, special thanks to the inspiring and encouraging Commissioning Editor Kristen Hammond, Senior Editor Alice Berry, Publicist Katie Elliott, Publishing Coordinator Keira de Hoog and Marketing Manager Peter Walmsley.

Writing a book takes time and energy and in my case that has only been possible because I have the amazing support of my family around me. Their perfectly timed cups of tea, delivered with a gentle non-interruptive placing of an encouraging hand on my shoulder, or the quiet whisper of 'dinner's ready' delivered as a smiling face appears around the edge of my study door, has enabled me to focus on writing.

Although my name appears on the front cover of this book, many people have contributed to the thinking and ideas contained in this book—people such as my customers, Thought Leader colleague and dear friend Matt Church, have offered continuous mentoring and encouragement over many years, all of which has significantly contributed to the development of my thinking and ideas. Thanks to my dear friend and colleague at Cultures At Work, Dougal Thompson, for his research, common sense advice and support and friendship.

I wish also to thank the many cynics and sceptics to my work that I have met along the way. Having my work scoffed at and belittled as being 'the soft stuff' is a useful experience to go through as it has taught me to think about the types of barriers to understanding that have to be overcome before a book like this can stand any chance of moving large numbers of people—in short they have helped me understand how to help even the most cynical to take culture seriously.

Finally I wish to thank my wife, Shar. If there is anyone that supports me to stay above the line it is Shar. Thank you for the thousands of conversations we have had together discussing every aspect of this work and this book. Your spirit, generosity, love and compassion for people is woven through every line written in this book. I love you.

Introduction

This book, as you have no doubt grasped from the front and back covers, is about creating a powerful and high-performance organisational culture. Culture is something I not only find fascinating, but also believe to be one of humanity's best inventions. Without culture, humanity would have failed to advance into civilisation. Culture is, for most of the billions of people on this planet, such a natural phenomenon that they could not imagine life without it. Culture offers humans a variety of powerful and inspiring enrichments to their daily lives. It is the source of human beings' sense of belonging, connection, belief, identity, courage, collaboration, empathy, art, music, sport, recreation, charity, sharing, celebration and commiserations, traditions, symbols, rituals, myths and heroism, and, of course, stories. Culture is both the overarching framework of human connection with others and the underlying distinction of separateness from the surrounding environment. Given the pervasive and all-encompassing presence of culture in people's lives, it surprises me how few companies really understand and work with their cultures. Why is this? Well, as you read through this book, you will discover many reasons for that.

Why I wrote this book

One reason is worth addressing immediately, as it explains the primary reason why I have written this book. I believe that, on the whole, organisations don't like people! That sounds like a harsh assessment, doesn't it? Maybe even a ridiculous statement as, of course, organisations are designed to serve people, aren't they? People such as customers, shareholders—even employees. So is my assessment fair? Is it even true? I believe so and I shall explain why shortly. But for now let me explain why this observation has led to me writing a book about organisational culture.

When we don't like something we seek to control it, or at least our relationship with it. We seek to limit our exposure to the things we do not like. Imagine you don't like horror movies. You will seek to ensure you have limited or no exposure to horror movies. You might even avert your eyes when a trailer for a horror movie appears on your TV or cinema screen. Because, in my opinion, organisations do not actually like people, this results in them seeking to control people through the use of systems, processes, policies and the like. In seeking to control people, organisations often put a stranglehold on the culture and in doing so lose the most powerful and productive offering people can provide. I have written this book to remind organisations and leaders of the critical role people and culture play in contributing to an organisation's performance.

Organisations and people

So, as promised, let me explain what I mean by the statement 'Organisations don't like people'.

My impression is that many organisations (even those that claim to be in service of people) would prefer to operate without having to employ people, or serve them if they could, as long as they could still make money. Organisations, you see, are designed to be organised, and as a result prefer things to run smoothly, reliably, efficiently, productively, predictably, logically, repetitively, mechanically and rationally. Organisations use a variety of systems, processes and methods to ensure they do.

People, on the other hand, tend to vary considerably from these desired organisational traits. People are often paradoxical—saying one thing but doing another. Changeable: they were committed, but now they're not so sure. People are emotional: their moods can and do influence their behaviour and decisions. People prefer stories to numbers: they will often ask what story the numbers are telling them in order to put the numbers into perspective. People are philosophical and even metaphysical: they put as much emphasis on and interest in what is unseen or not measurable. They believe in luck, synchronicity, fate, karma, destiny — or they don't, but the people working alongside them, and across the counter, do.

From an organisation's perspective, human beings are messy. They are excitable or unsure, courageous or afraid, passionate or bored — in short, they are human.

To cope with the nature of people being human, organisations have developed a series of mechanisms to attempt to control the organic nature of people. They have implemented such things as human resource systems, people measurement, management roles, contracts and conditions, survey profiling, training and disciplinary procedures. All of which tend to achieve two distinct outcomes. First, they signal to employees that the organisation doesn't really trust them. Second, they signal in a subtle manner that the organisation doesn't really like them.

I'm not sure when organisations reached the point where they began to see and plan for people being a nuisance, but at some stage it happened. Is every organisation like this? No, of course not. Is your organisation like this? Hopefully not. But just to be sure, maybe you should check, as in my experience more organisations are like this than not. Next time you interact with an organisation, perhaps at your local supermarket, bank, petrol station, tax department, hospital, courier service or restaurant, pay attention to the extent to which these organisations seem to appreciate, enjoy or even celebrate people. I hope, I really hope, that some of them do. I expect, however, that many will not. Organisations don't mean to be this way. They didn't set out to not like people. 'We don't like people' are not words you will find written into their vision or mission statement, or in any expression of their values. In fact, I'm sure you will find quite the opposite. But, in reality, in the act of delivering their service or employing their staff, or managing their business, somehow, the enjoyment and celebration of people is quickly forgotten under the demand for efficiency, effectiveness, timeliness and profits.

If you can begin to sense that not only is there some truth in this idea that organisations don't like people, you also will realise that this is somewhat ironic, given that organisations are fundamentally here to employ and serve people. There are, of course, organisations that take people to their hearts and place them at the centre of their endeavours. Many of these organisations fully commit to working with their people to ensure the workplace is a positive experience, which in turn enables employees to be at their best for the customer's sake. Often, however, despite the organisation's best attempts to improve the workplace experience for employees, their approaches inadvertently work against getting the very outcome they are committed to achieving.

I value organisations

It might be worthwhile pausing at this stage to point out that I am not (as it may appear) anti-organisation. I'm just tired of seeing them failing to integrate effectively with human beings, whether as employees, customers, shareholders or stakeholders. I am, in fact, very pro-organisation, and I have written this book to support them, to more effectively inspire employees to create and sustain a culture that provides the organisation with increased performance. In the 21st century, it is the commercially oriented organisations with empowered and high-performance cultures that will so often have the necessary influence, capital, power and opportunity to serve people and really make a difference. When was the last time you saw a politician anywhere in the world make a bold, decisive, significant and positive change to the status quo? I can count them on one hand.

This need to reconnect with the idea that people matter to organisations is a key theme in this book. When you start with the premise that people matter, then you quickly begin to see that culture also matters. This is because, whenever a group of people spend regular time together in a location, a culture will emerge. This does not have to be planned, as it will happen organically. However, when a culture is deliberately developed and nurtured, it becomes stronger and more sustainable. If this strength of the culture is aligned to a business strategy then you can expect very high levels of performance to follow.

This book offers a tried and tested way of connecting the people in your organisation with its culture, which in turn can be aligned to your business strategy to generate maximum benefit for all.

Above the line culture

An *above the line culture* is one in which the people in the culture (employees and leaders) create for themselves a positive and inspiring environment. An above the line culture also provides delight to customers, shareholders, employees' families, suppliers, and the board of directors.

A *below the line* culture is a culture that doesn't work. By 'doesn't work' I mean the culture is ineffective, toxic or even dead. Any of these conditions lead to people suffering. Cultures are all about people (by the people, for the people), and not delivering optimum experiences for people renders them not working or below the line. By the time we are through this book we shall of course come to understand above and below the line in depth, but for now just think of above the line as a positive, productive experience for people and below the line as not!

This book offers a workable, fun and engaging approach to enhancing organisational culture. The approach delivers a very practical, easy-to-implement method for inspiring a high-performance culture that engages employees and delights customers.

The approach to working with culture presented here is quite different from the approaches typically adopted by organisations. My approach places a significant emphasis on developing an understanding of what culture actually is, before launching into doing anything about changing it.

This book will give you the tools to move far beyond the common platitudes, such as 'Culture is the way we do things around here' or 'Our values are our culture'. Or such limited descriptions of culture as, 'We have a collaborative culture'. Too many organisations do not understand the nature and structure of culture and end up investing time, money, energy and people in attempts to change, grow or replicate the culture. This seems a little redundant when we consider how a company can expect to achieve great results, working with something as complex as culture, if it does not first understand what culture actually is. Yet the overwhelming majority of organisations that attempt to work on their culture do not actually understand culture in its full capacity and influence.

The importance of culture

When clients ask for my suggestions on what to work on or improve their culture my first rule is 'First, understand culture and its importance', and only then can you plan accordingly. Of course, many businesspeople do not know much about culture because they do not understand its significance, or they falsely assume they have got by just fine until now without needing to know too much about it. In fact, some even still query if culture has any real role to play in the performance of their organisation, and often assume that the current focus and intense activity being placed on creating powerful workplace cultures is just a passing trend.

So the question is whether all this emphasis on culture is just the latest business trend. I always answer this question with the same answer. 'No, business is just the latest cultural trend.'

People seem to forget that human beings have been embracing culture as a way of working and living together far longer than business has existed. Culture is ancient. Business is in its infancy by comparison—especially modern business and specifically the model of the corporation, which was invented when, in 1600, Queen Elizabeth I granted a royal charter to England's East India Company. The point being that if you truly wish to master running a successful business, it would pay (often handsomely) to understand the very DNA of what enables people to function together collectively and effectively—which is to understand the ancient human invention that is the very foundation of every organisation: culture.

Expecting and encouraging a group of human beings to work together over a long time means a culture will emerge, and it will be required to harness the collective belief and energy of the group. In fact, the organisation, with its strategy, structure, shareholders and marketplace, will not be able to stop a culture forming, regardless of how the business is performing. Why is this? Human beings are wired for culture. In his fascinating book *Wired for Culture: The Natural History of Human Cooperation*, Mark Pagel, head of the evolution laboratory at the School of Biological Sciences at the University of Reading in England, describes just how powerfully connected humans are to culture. Pagel suggests that, as a species, we invented culture for ourselves some 160 000 to 200 000 years ago. He describes how humans acquired the ability to copy and imitate, even improve upon, behaviours and actions from one generation to the next, and says that this ability gave us a significant evolutionary advantage over other species. The various elements of culture could be transferred, in much the same way that genes enable physical characteristics to be transferred from one generation to the next. However, the elements of culture, such as beliefs, traditions, techniques, technology, art, songs, language and traditions, could all be adapted and improved upon, in a way genes could not.

Culture and evolution

This ability to transfer units of culture, often called memes, extended the usual system of inheritance from relying exclusively on genes. Pagel says this ability changed everything.

> Our cultural heritage is something we take for granted today, but its invention forever altered the course of evolution and our world. This is because knowledge could accumulate as good ideas were retained, combined, and improved upon, and others were discarded.

Pagel suggests that this process of culturing also enabled us to adopt faster:

> And, being able to jump from mind to mind granted the elements of culture a pace of change that stood in relation to our genetical evolution something like an animal's behaviour does to a more leisurely movement of a plant.

Pagel explains that culture quickly became the dominant source of our evolutionary progress, as we could learn to adapt during the course of a single lifetime and escape the restrictions we may have encountered from the biological inheritance of our genes. Consequently, culture 'outstripped our genes in providing solutions to the problems of our existence'. Pagel suggests this ability to escape from the inherited restrictions of our genes is a significant advantage in terms not only of survival but also adaptation and prosperity. As humans, we are the only species that can acquire and learn the rules of survival through daily life and knowledge transferred from our ancestors, rather than simply through the genes they passed on to us. This knowledge could be extended and added to significantly in just one lifetime, meaning that over three generations a knowledge base could be enhanced significantly, whereas the genetic code remained the same.

What all this means is that culture became a human strategy for survival. No other species has this social adaptation system to rely on for adaptation. Organisations need to understand this inbuilt condition for humans to be wired for culture. In my experience, not many do. It is important because it explains why humans will always rely on culture to create a sense of belonging through which to nurture, grow and protect themselves. A business strategy, by comparison, lacks this emotive, hardwired connection for most employees. As culture is hardwired, you may have begun to realise that, for a strategy to be initiated and then executed, it must first be accepted by the very culture from which it is hoping to draw its energy and activity. People are wired for culture, but will debate and renege on a strategy based on their culture's immune system.

A culture is built upon a set of values and beliefs. Any business strategy that is at odds with these values and beliefs is doomed, as culture will always prove to be a more powerful attraction for people, because it is hardwired. Strategy, by comparison, is soft wired. People will go along with a strategy only as long as it serves their cultural purposes. People also create a culture around a sense of identity, which a strategy may offer but too often does not. If the strategy is at odds with how the people see themselves, the strategy will again be rejected by the culture. Sometimes this rejection is formal and therefore easily recognised by the senior leaders of the organisation, but more often the business strategy is rejected informally, meaning it is subtly sabotaged over a period of weeks, months and years, through a variety of mechanisms including:

- staff withholding ideas and suggestions
- high turnover in staff
- lack of commitment
- lack of collaboration
- lack of application
- increased absenteeism
- breakdown in communication
- punctuality issues
- quality issues.

All these, and more, are symptoms of a culture rejecting its organisation's business strategy or leadership. Because culture is hardwired and influential, it is critical that organisations learn to master the ability to inspire a culture that will align with their business objectives.

This book is the result of a lifetime's work of studying culture and understanding what really works and what does not when it comes to developing a workplace culture. In particular, I will outline how to understand culture, why it is so important to do so, and finally what to do in terms of planning your organisation's culture. This book offers a change of direction for those leaders and organisations still relying on external providers of culture climate and engagement surveys, and in doing so puts the understanding of culture back into its rightful hands: those of the people who actually work in the culture.

This belief that culture belongs to the people who work in it is one of many I have come to subscribe to as I have observed the difference between above the line and below the line cultures. Although I describe it as a belief, I do not mean that I am making this opinion up, but rather that I am convinced of it from decades of field work and observation. There are many more beliefs that I subscribe to or have formulated in this manner as I created the above the line culture approach. You might even say I have become hardwired around these beliefs, and so it is only fair that I share them with you and make them as transparent as possible before you read further. Many providers of culture methodologies do not openly declare their underlying beliefs and assumptions to their customers, for fear of being rejected on the grounds of mismatching beliefs. This has always struck me as somewhat ironic, as beliefs and perspectives form a powerful and influential aspect of all cultures. These beliefs, when exposed and understood, hopefully explain why the author or designer of a culture process has chosen and favours that particular approach. This can be very insightful, as it enables leaders in organisations to go beyond simply the rational and logical efficiency offered by the culture approach or survey and begin to understand the emotive drivers hidden beneath the approach. Such beliefs are the hidden reason that the developers of the approach were motivated to design their approach the way they have. Common examples of such beliefs might include:

- applying a theory is preferred to observing reality, because a theory is supposed to be more objective in its approach, especially if offered from a supplier with an academic background

- taking a religious persuasion approach: favouring a religious or spiritual approach to viewing how organisations should operate

- taking a psychological perspective: what works for individuals applies to groups and culture

- relying on cultural or geographical background, such as a northern hemisphere, or Western or Eastern perspective

- using a metaphorical reference: think of the company as a machine, or tribe, or brain or military unit.

I wish to be as transparent as possible in what I am offering in this approach, and explain why I feel motivated to do so. To achieve this, I have listed the beliefs underpinning my work.

Supporting beliefs

The underlying beliefs inspiring this book and my approach to culture include the following.

- Culture underscores every human endeavour and activity in the workplace.

- Culture is one of the best inventions of human beings, but not enough organisations understand this or tap into the immense power a culture offers.

- Every organisation has a culture, whether it knows it or not. The trick is to know it and act accordingly.

- Culture has more influence on an organisation's performance than strategy. Strategy is important, but aligning the culture to the strategy is even more important.

- Business strategy without an aligned culture is powerless.

- Company culture without a business strategy meanders.

- Culture is dynamic not static.

- Culture belongs to people, not the organisation.

- The size and location of an organisation affects its culture.

- Deliberate conscious culturing is powerful. The word 'culturing' implies the dedicated ongoing focus on the wellbeing and growth of a culture.

- People's personal values are more important than organisational values.

- Work is a privilege.

- You cannot work with and influence culture if you do not understand it.

- Staff engagement surveys do not measure cultures.

- People are what make change possible — or impossible.

- People want to do well at work. Most people, in my experience, wish to do good, be good and serve others. Let's back these people with our culture systems and processes, rather than have the minority of people who are not aligned in this manner dictate our culture and systems.

- People's personal values are more important for an organisation's performance than the company values. An alignment of both is best.

- Values can and do change. Even company values can become outdated.

- Leadership is not a title. Ironically, only bad leaders think leadership is a title.

- Too many leaders are under-trained and promoted into roles they are not ready for or not supported enough to develop the necessary skills to cope with something as complex as a high-performance culture.

- When done well (and to quote Michael Port), business is a love story disguised as a strategy.

- Culture is available in two forms: above and below the line.

These beliefs of mine about culture also seem to be present in most above the line cultures. Not all occur in every culture, but enough of them to warrant your being aware of them in case they can serve you or your organisation. There are many more beliefs, both mine and those embodied within above the line cultures, discussed throughout the book, which I openly declare and even highlight to ensure you do not miss them. However, I suggest you evaluate their worth in the context of your interest in your own culture.

Finally, I am aware you may not have come across a business book written by a corporate anthropologist before. Although they are numerous in North America and Europe, corporate anthropologists are a rare breed in Australasia, and so I have decided to provide the following short introduction to how, as a corporate anthropologist, I approach my work of supporting organisations to create powerful workplace cultures.

A corporate anthropologist at work

I have relied predominantly on the anthropology practices of participant observation and ethnography as the key means to uncovering insights about culture. I then take these insights and learning, and share them with organisations.

If you are new to these terms let me quickly explain what they are and how they work.

Participant observation

As the words themselves describe, participant observation is a process of working with people and, while doing so, simultaneously observing what people are doing, how they go about doing what they are doing, and paying deep attention to the language they use to communicate with one another and customers. This process enables an anthropologist to begin to explore, understand and gain familiarity with the observable level of culture. Gaining familiarity can require the anthropologist to ask a lot of questions of the people that they themselves might easily find simplistic or obvious or even stupid. For example, much of the jargon that organisations use, although very familiar to people within the organisation or profession, can be completely alien to someone outside of the company or profession. An example of a word that needed to be explained to me is 'ward'. I heard this word being referred to regularly when I was studying the culture of a business in the insurance industry. I asked them what it meant. It turns out that a previous employee, who had been negligent in filing a claim for a customer, had ended up causing a considerable amount of unnecessary heartache for the client and expense for the company. The individual's surname was Ward. So whenever people were referring to a project or case that, if not treated with a lot of attention to detail, could become a problem out of proportion to the actual claim size, the situation was labelled a 'ward'!

Participant observation requires the anthropologist to pay attention to artefacts and symbols and identify the underlying values and beliefs. These symbols can include a wide range of items including:

- company values
- safety charts and instructions on the wall
- motivational poster or messages
- directional information
- personal pictures, quotes, cartoons or jokes
- vision, mission or project statements
- warnings and reminders
- menus or recipes for procedures
- tools
- furniture
- awards
- team names or colours
- art
- music
- charts
- technology
- manuals
- reference books
- catalogues.

Ethnographic field work

Ethnography is just a fancy word for capturing a people's story. 'Ethno' is from the root word in Greek for race, while the word 'graphic' is a picture or telling of a tale, as in autobiographic. Ethnographic field work involves an anthropologist visiting the culture in person (rather than reading about it in a book or on a website), and engaging in a variety of activities and conversations in an attempt to understand the deeper meaning and significance of the culture. The techniques used in this process can include:

- observation
- informal conversations
- formal question and answer sessions
- interviews and reviews of individuals' accounts of their life and work in the culture
- gathering data or statistical data
- mapping a physical environment
- surveys
- photography and videotaping to capture images of symbols, work and ceremonies.

Often the anthropologist will work with a person or small group of people from within the culture to act as interpreters, not just of language if the anthropologist is unfamiliar with the jargon or terms used, but also to delve into the deeper significance of the observations and conversations, rituals or behaviours they witness.

Anyway, enough about anthropology, let's get on with the target of anthropology, which is of course to understand culture.

Understanding culture

To help you understand the various cultures that are described in this book, I have deliberately tried to avoid offering too many case study examples or 'benchmarks', as is common in most business books providing models of excellence. This is for two important reasons.

First, you can't benchmark culture! You might like to think of culture as operating more as a verb than a noun. Culture is an active process of being and doing that occurs in a very organic and dynamic manner. One not easily replicated. Culture comprises as much, some would say more, of the intangible as the tangible. So when it comes to culture, to offer a sample benchmark is a little misleading and offers unfair expectations for anyone simply trying to copy 'what they did' and expect the same results.

Culture is not a formulaic process or business system that has embedded within it a machine-like conformity and consistency. Every culture is unique! Failure to understand this point can lead to organisations spending huge amounts of time, money and effort trying to copy another culture when in reality this simply is not possible. Nor should you try to copy a culture. One of the most important keys to really powerful cultures is the fact that they are unique!

I recall many years ago working with a fast food business that had franchises across Australasia, and the CEO had asked me to replicate the culture from the best restaurants in the chain in the vast majority of the others, which were lagging. It took some time to explain to the CEO that culture isn't created in the same way that the organisation's famous flagship burgers were. I explained to him that, unlike the carefully designed recipe for their delicious burgers, the very careful construction and layout of each ingredient in the burger—which were placed meticulously to ensure the customer, no matter where they bit into the burger, accessed enough of the core ingredients to experience a consistent taste as they devoured the burger—did not apply to culture. For a moment or two he looked at me and frowned as if baffled by how this could possibly be so. After a while a glimmer of insight swept across his face and he said hesitantly, 'Because the people in the culture of each restaurant are all different, right?' I nodded in response and, as this realisation sunk deeper into his understanding, he smiled and threw his hands up in a gesture of genuine surprise and surrender, and said, 'Okay, Mr Anthropologist, show me what we have to do.'

The second reason for believing you are wasting your time benchmarking your culture against others is that cultures change. I've been amused that some books that were considered to be the epitome of best practice at the time of publication, or that provided world-class examples of organisations who had got things right (*Good to Great* by Jim Collins and *In Search of Excellence* by Tom Peters come to mind) were subsequently criticised by the media for being false prophets, as many of the organisations held up as shining examples of excellence are in fact no longer in business. They have either been taken over as part of a merger or acquisition, been wound up or gone bankrupt. The argument by the book critics is that the authors got things wrong, that their theories were flawed or that their ideas were just the latest trend.

I understand this perspective; I just do not agree with it. At the time, the evidence, research and circumstances the authors were observing seemed to validate their thinking. The fact that the world changes around these organisations or that the leadership teams changed or that the culture didn't allow for the necessary adaption could not have been anticipated, and to expect that they could have is perhaps naive. The particular reason I found this critical response amusing was that the critics had no understanding or empathy for the authors or the organisations that had disappeared. So although the recipe for success looked sound at the time of the research, the authors, the organisations, and perhaps even the critics, could not have foreseen the fact that the necessary cultural ingredients for success would move or be taken away. In summary, to think that an organisation is replicable is fine, up to a point. But to not include the intangible, paradoxical nature of human beings and change as part of your expectations means that the authors and the critics were not wrong in their commentary as such: they were simply limited in the contextual setting from which their observations, theories and commentaries were being drawn.

My intent for this book is to remind you of the importance of culture. To share with you the power of culture. To reclaim the core of business as an intent by one group of people to serve others. To celebrate culture as the wonderful invention that it is, that has given our species the survival and competitive advantage it has and to transport this into the realms of our modern organisations.

I hope you enjoy the read. I hope it inspires and enables you to act with deliberate intent for your culture, as not to do so would be to waste an opportunity to engage with what I consider to be one of human beings' best inventions — culture!

Michael Henderson
July 2014

Part I

UNDERSTANDING CULTURE

EXCELLING

SUCCESSFUL

STABLE

DYING

DEAD

CHAPTER 1

What is culture?

When I was still an undergraduate student studying anthropology, my professor shared a story with the class. He described how, at the end of every work day, Soviet Union factory workers would be stopped at the gates and searched to ensure they were not stealing any of Mother Russia's resources or tools. One particular worker, who had formed the daily habit of pushing a wheelbarrow home, would watch patiently as the armed guards searched through the wheelbarrow, burrowing through the work coat, thick wool vest and food basket it contained. Finding no stolen items, the guards would wave the worker on his way. After several years the worker suddenly stopped turning up to work. It was later discovered, much to the delighted amusement and admiration of many of his comrades, that he had been stealing wheelbarrows from the factory. He had then sold them to local farmers and in this way been able to save up enough money to bribe the appropriate officials and escape from the Soviet Union.

The professor shared this story to highlight to his anthropology students just how easy it can be to stare straight at something, even on a daily basis, and still not register or understand its true significance. He suggested that, as anthropology students, we would probably find ourselves in just this situation as we went travelling about the world looking for cultures to study. He was right. Learning to identify a culture is no easy task. It takes patience, depth of insight and an ability to appreciate the sub-text of the exhibited language (verbal, physical and symbolic). Learning to not simply stare at a culture without truly perceiving its deeper significance is a skill set that can take years to develop.

In my experience many, maybe even most, people inside an organisation find themselves in exactly the same situation as the guards at the gates of the Soviet factory regarding their own company culture. They are staring straight at the culture on a daily basis and yet still fail to register or understand its true significance. The company culture, just like the wheelbarrow at the factory gates, is passing before people in the organisation every day, but they are often too busy looking at other things to register its significance. So although, when you know what to look for, aspects of a culture are apparent in every meeting, production line, conversation with a customer, training and planning session, health and safety debriefing, induction program, interview and performance feedback, culture itself goes largely unnoticed.

Defining culture

It makes sense in a book about culture that we take a moment to define the word 'culture'. No doubt you have heard people in your organisation regularly use the word. But what is it we are referring to when we speak of culture?

Next time you hear someone use the word, stop and ask them what they actually mean. You might be surprised by the answers they provide. Many people use the word 'culture' without having any real depth of understanding of what the word actually means. This is completely understandable, because most people working in organisations have not studied culture in any formal manner.

It is important, if you want to inspire and lead a culture, that you first understand what culture is. It is also useful to hear how people currently define culture. I have learnt that asking people what they mean when they use the word 'culture' can provide insights into how they are relating to and interpreting the wheelbarrow.

The way of culture

The most common way I hear culture described is as 'the way we do things around here'. I'm sure you too have heard people refer to culture in this way. So how does this definition of culture inform us of people's understanding of culture? Let's explore this.

To start with, 'the way we do things around here' is a completely understandable description of culture by people who have never really thought about or tried to understand culture, because on the surface that is exactly what culture looks like. But if you take a closer look at the words 'the way we do things around here', you will realise that it better describes the delivery of a business strategy than it does company culture.

The use of the word 'way' places the emphasis on process. A process is a way of doing something and it is designed to deliver a final outcome. While process is a part of culture, it is only a small part. When we focus on the *way* of culture, we overlook the who, why, where and when of culture.

In other words, when an organisation describes its culture as 'the way we do things around here', it reveals a limited awareness of only a part of what creates a culture and makes it great. The part consists of the most obvious, observable, tactical and measurable aspects of company culture. However, to ignore the other parts of culture means we achieve only a partial understanding of the more complex and powerful entity that is culture.

In a moment we will explore and determine a deeper understanding of culture and reveal how much more there is to culture. In fact, you could accurately argue that the phrase 'the way we do things around here' better describes strategy than culture.

The why of culture

Culture is not the *way* we do things so much as the *why*. '*Why* we do things this way around here' is a far better definition of culture. This definition captures the importance and powerful, motivating aspect of understood meaning. Put another way, when people know *why* they are doing something, they are far more likely to feel compelled to engage in their given activities with everything they have to offer. This is especially true if, once the why is contemplated and understood, the concept speaks to the individual's deepest personal values.

Understanding why the *way* is, as it is, is an essential part of culture production. Traditional tribes that have managed to maintain their cultures for thousands of years go to great lengths to ensure that all members understand the why behind the rituals, traditions and day-to-day processes embodied within their culture. When tribe members make this connection for themselves, they do not require any further micromanagement, 360-degree feedback or performance appraisals to ensure they are doing things the right way. Each person's conscience becomes his or her leader, guiding the way from the communal motivation of why. When people describe culture in terms of why things are done a certain way it signals that they understand that culture is not just surface level. It's bone deep, blood deep, and includes and activates a powerful underlying sense of meaning and a source of great motivation. In modern organisations, to ignore or remain naive about this deeper aspect of culture leads to seeing the wheelbarrow as simple a way of moving things from one place to another, rather than coming to a deeper understanding by seeing the wheelbarrow for its real significance — seeing it as currency.

My recommendation, then, is to ensure that, before you begin any cultural change or transformation program in or across your organisation, you first pause to check what people's understanding of the word culture is. Failure to do so can lead to your executives focusing the change effort on only the surface level of culture, which unfortunately will look as though it has been successful over a short period of time. The deeper, unnoticed and unappreciated aspects of culture will, however, announce their presence and influence before long, meaning that the shallower surface changes will quickly be jeopardised and the organisation's people will begin to revert to previous behaviours or begin to morph into unplanned-for and unexpected new behaviours.

A formal definition of culture

You will be hard-pressed to find a universally accepted definition of culture. Even anthropologists can't agree on a definition. Whenever

I'm pressed to provide a formal definition of culture I usually say something like this:

> Culture is an active, self-questioning and –organising process of shared personal values, beliefs and rituals that creates meaning that is transmitted from one generation to another through learned formal and informal interactions that occur daily.

I will be the first to admit that that is quite a mouthful. If you are interested in understanding in more detail what this definition means and how, by understanding its various parts, you can quickly deepen your own insight into culture, then simply read through the following paragraphs and I will explain each aspect of the definition one at a time. If, however, you are happy with this definition and simply wish to move on, then jump ahead to the next section in this chapter, 'A simpler definition of culture'. In the meantime, let's review the definition I have just provided. Let's start at the beginning.

Culture is active and self-organising

To understand culture and to move far beyond the limitations of thinking of culture as being only 'the way we do things around here', you must grasp this point that culture is active and self-organising. Too often organisations relate to their culture as if they were dealing with a stationary object, or something that is fixed in time. For example, some years ago a CEO said to me, 'Oh yeah, we've done culture. We did it last year. There it is on the wall.' She pointed to a mission statement and a set of values that hung framed on a nearby wall.

The CEO falsely assumed several things:

- The culture was likely to still the same as it was when the wording had been completed.
- Culture is and can be captured as a set of words.
- Work on culture can reach a point of conclusion.

To assume a culture is static is dangerous. In fact anthropologists have noted that, when a culture becomes static, it is at risk, as it can fail to adjust to the world or environment changing around it. To accommodate a more agile view of culture, I encourage all of my clients to think about, and use, the word 'culturing' instead of just using the word 'culture'.

Culturing

By culturing I mean that the people in the organisation are constantly and deliberately working with the culture to enhance their awareness of its role and the consequences for the business and customers. I have had a number of clients tell me that, once they began to think and speak of the word 'culturing', it made everyone more aware of the culture's presence in everything they were doing. In using the word 'culturing' we constantly remind ourselves that culture is always in the process of becoming something. Culturing is mutable, complex, journeying, evolving and perpetually expanding or shrinking. Throughout this book I will use both the word 'culture' when naming the process of social interaction inside organisations, and the word 'culturing' when I wish to remind you of the deliberate approach to inspiring and working with culture.

Changing the way we think about culture, from something static to something active that is constantly developing and changing, means we do not fall into the all-too-common trap of administering a 'culture change program' and then checking the 'company culture' off our to-do lists. Culture is never complete. In fact, all the changes within an organisation — tactical, strategic, structural, geographical or technological — are culturing changes. If your organisation becomes accustomed to thinking of culturing instead of culture, your employees will be more readily able to consider the impact of corporate-sanctioned change on company culturing. For example, your company might consider how a new technological change within the database system, or the decision to replace water coolers with water bottles, affects company culturing.

Much to the consternation of many a culture-change project leader, culturing is not necessarily contained in the change management plan. Culturing is self-organising. If you think of culture as a collective response to circumstances and simultaneously consider that circumstances regularly change, you can begin to see how culture is forced to self-organise and evolve. Any initiatives launched by an organisation—a product launch, a merger, the introduction of a new leader, upgraded technology, or the downsizing or upsizing of the business—will always inspire a response from company culture. In very simple terms, the company culture will either accept or reject these changes. Leadership can (and should) attempt to shift the odds in the direction of approving—just don't assume compliance or acceptance will happen automatically simply because you generated a change management plan.

Culture is shared values, beliefs and rituals

Let's start this next part of the breakdown of my formal definition of culture by looking at the notion of shared values. In this case I am not referring to morals, which tend to be about judgements or delineating right from wrong. I am also not referring to ethics, which are mostly about an agreed-upon code of behaviour shared by a specific group. Instead, I am talking about values as the personal preferences and priorities that underscore our decision making, motivation and meaning-making. A set of shared values is not so much about agreeing that we all value integrity—who in their right mind would publicly admit to feeling any other way, anyway? Values are more about each of us digging deep within ourselves to truly understand our own unique set of personal preferences and priorities. These can then be shared with other members of the tribe through decision making, story swapping, goal setting and behaviour. The point is that organisations are often too quick to create a set of values that read like Shakespearian poetry or a rallying call by former British prime minister Winston Churchill:

> We, in our commitment to humility, outstanding service and integrity, dedicate all of our efforts to making sure that all stakeholders receive nurturing, world-class service that at once strengthens our own efforts and the efforts of the entire, sentient-being-filled universe.

While companies may claim to value people's efforts and ideals, the truth is that the real values of any organisation are the ones commonly considered to have high priority among the people who work in the company. Truly understanding what values your people bring to work every day will give the company a far greater ability to work with people where they are and inspire them to move forward as part of the collective. The best way to discover the real values at work within a culture is not to read them on the wall of the office canteen or reception, but to watch what people prioritise above all else in their everyday work! Having considered the values aspect of the description of culture, we'll move onto beliefs.

Where values express what is most important to us through preferences and priorities, beliefs define why the values are important to us. A belief is best described as someone's degree of certainty about something. For example, if people believe that a project is not worthy of their best efforts, it is unlikely, no matter how much management interferes with people's work on a daily basis in an effort to lift their performance, that the individuals will ever give their best. If others who share the same belief and the same degree of certainty about that belief join any individual holding the belief, the collective ease and conviction in believing becomes even easier. The shared beliefs within an organisation can massively influence the performance of people in the business. Belief is powerful. Very powerful. So a key role of leadership is to pay attention to the beliefs people have within the business. It is always better to have people's beliefs working for your company, and not against it.

The role of rituals in culture

Rituals are an integral and powerful aspect of culture. Some are formalised, such as a company's departure ceremony, promotion celebration or sales awards. Some are not: Friday lunchtime card games, happy hour rounds on the boss after a sales surge, doughnuts for the office from the 'new guy' after his first week. The careful encouragement and discouragement of various rituals will add enormous amounts of flavour and inspiration to your company culture. Rituals bring sumptuousness and meaning to your culturing. By sumptuousness I mean that rituals highlight culture through the involvement of all six senses: seeing, hearing, smelling, tasting, touching and feeling make our culturing experience feel real and alive. Rituals bring meaning to your culture because they employ and embody symbolic representation of the tribe's deepest values. The more deliberate and consistent a tribe becomes in its engagement with formal rituals, the more that tribe is able to solidify the collective beliefs and core values that they wish to embody in their daily behaviours.

If you have never done so, take time over the next few weeks to observe the informal rituals in your workplace culture. Who shares the morning newspaper? Who brings coffee or orders lunch? Where do people congregate to share information, discuss and solve problems, or gripe about the latest sports team loss? Observe the rituals associated with the meetings you hold. Where do people sit? Who speaks? More importantly, who listens?

Culture is shared meaning-making

For me everything culturing achieves boils down to these three words: shared meaning-making. Most traditional cultures and tribes would nod in agreement over the importance of these words. Most modern organisations, however, will need further explanation.

Think about this. What does working for your organisation mean to the people working there? When I ask this question of organisation leaders, they usually reply with a list of wonderful things like this: a chance to work for a big brand or market leader; opportunities for development/travel/promotion; potential for upward-mobility. You get the idea.

What's interesting is that I have asked this question of hundreds of senior leaders in hundreds of organisations and they have always painted a wonderful picture of their organisation. Yet when I ask the same question of staff members within those organisations, I get a more mixed response: long hours, glass ceilings, mediocre pay, putting up with an incompetent boss, high stress levels, not enough recognition, too much time away from the family, broken promises, and no clear picture of where we are going. Again, you get the picture.

I believe that knowing what it means to work for your organisation is an important step in understanding how your company culturing needs to improve. I often advise my clients that what matters most is not the work people do, but what that work means to them. The more a leader is able to identify and articulate the meaning people make about the organisation's intent, policy, system or process, the easier it is for the leader to align people's efforts to the strategy or communicate in a way that draws upon people's sense of meaning. It can also help a leader to reconsider and adjust a policy to people, to better accommodate people's sense of meaning. Meaning matters. Meaning motivates. Lack of meaning doesn't! To finish let's examine the final aspect of my formal definition of culture.

Culture is transmitted from generation to generation

Traditionally we think of the word 'generation' as referring to an age group — the sons and daughters growing up, ready to take over the responsibilities of day-to-day living and the future direction of the family culture. A generation occurs every 20 years or so. In modern organisations, however, a generation can occur every quarter or every six months, simply through the mobility, and the coming and going of staff. Paying attention to generational shifts is important to culture because a culture is passed from one generation of your tribe to the next. Here is a story that explains how.

An experiment was conducted with five monkeys kept in a cage. A bunch of bananas was hung from the roof of the cage, with a stable ladder placed beneath it. It didn't take long before a monkey moved towards the ladder to reach for the bananas. However, the moment the monkey touched the ladder, a cold jet of water squirted out at all the other monkeys. After a while, another monkey tried to climb the ladder, but the group experienced the same results: all the other monkeys were sprayed with cold water. Before long, any monkey approaching the ladder was screamed at by the others as a warning and immediately stopped and changed direction away from the ladder. The band had learned the consequences of touching the ladder.

Next, the water jets were removed and one monkey from the cage was replaced with a new one. The new monkey saw the bananas and wanted to climb the ladder. To his surprise and horror, all of the other monkeys screamed at him the moment he got close to the ladder.

After another attempt and further screaming, he quickly learned not to go anywhere near the ladder.

Next, another of the original monkeys was removed and again a new monkey was sent into the cage as a replacement. Just like the previous new monkey, this new monkey attempted to go for the bananas only to be screamed at by the band. Interestingly, even the previous new monkey took part in the screaming with as much vigour as the original monkeys! The replacement of one original monkey with a new one was continued until all the original monkeys were replaced. Every time the newest monkey approached the ladder, it was reprimanded. Even though none of the remaining monkeys had ever been sprayed with cold water, they all still screamed at any monkey who approached the ladder to try for the bananas.

I don't know if this experiment actually took place, but it is certainly a useful metaphor to draw similarities to human behaviour in modern organisations, because in organisations culture is transmitted from one generation to another.

I have a wonderful client with a 70-year company heritage. The CEO is rightly very proud of the organisation's history and growth. Interestingly, and understandably, he was a little confused to hear some of his senior colleagues expressing their belief that the company culture was just the same as it had been when the company started. He asked the human resources manager to present the senior leadership team with some enlightening data. It was revealed that over 50 per cent of the thousands of people in the organisation had been in the company for only two years. With that percentage of new people contributing to the workplace culture, the leadership team was awakened to the possibility that the culture had most likely become something completely different than they had known even 20 years ago. I was given a contract to map the company culturing as it appeared in the present rather than simply assuming the culture was still the same as it had been 70 years ago. Understandably the culture had evolved and changed significantly due to a wide range of factors, including new developments in technology, a growth in branches from one nation to many, ongoing changes in leadership teams and business strategies, political and economic changes around the world and the changing demands of their global clients.

Part of my report to the senior leaders highlighted that when culture is being transmitted from one generation to another, it is possible, as in their own case, that the newest generation is in fact the group most likely to be doing the most prolific transmitting. The 50 per cent of the organisation's people who had joined in the past two years held a more common view and understanding of the organisation's culture than those who had arrived over the previous 68 years. So clearly the culture in the modern age is not the same as that which was formed in the organisation's early days.

Having explored all the separate parts of this definition of culture, let's quickly put them back together again so that you can consolidate your understanding.

> Culture is an active, self-questioning and organising process of shared personal values, beliefs and rituals that creates meaning that is transmitted from one generation to another through learned formal and informal interactions that occur daily.

If you still find this a little confusing or overwhelming, try the following.

A simpler definition of culture

You might like to consider a simpler and all-encompassing version I often use in my keynotes when I do not have the time to explain the more detailed version.

My short definition is in two parts and the first goes like this: Culture is what it means to be human here! If I work in your organisation what is expected of me? What am I expected to believe in? Hard work? Profit making? Customer service? Team work? What am I required to sacrifice? Time with my family? Energy for my hobbies and recreational preferences? Who or what do I become as a result of working here? Happier, more energised, fulfilled, creative or collaborative? Or something different: fatigued, cynical, isolated, alienated or saddened? Asking yourself what does it mean to be human here, and then taking the time to observe and listen to people as they go about their daily work over a period of time, allows the answers to come to you. An understanding of culture will always emerge if you're patient enough to wait for it, and you know what to look or listen for. Usually within a period of fewer than three weeks you will begin to perceive and hear the answers to your question, and perhaps even be able to formulate an answer.

I ask myself the question 'What does it mean to be human here?' on every visit to every client, and in doing so allow the culture to reveal itself to me. It may seem like a rather simplistic approach, but it's the simplicity that I like about it. It also allows the culture to just become apparent. No need for surveys, focus groups or pre-scripted questions in search of premeditated answers. No. Asking myself 'What does it mean to be human here?' and then just watching and listening for the answer has proven to be not only accurate but also incredibly insightful, providing a level of understanding and clarity that would otherwise go unnoticed.

The second part of my simple definition of culture is this: 'Culturing is what turns a person into a people.' Since the dawn of humans' time on this planet, culture is what has enabled each person to surrender a purely egotistical drive in order to satisfy the equally strong drive and human need to belong. Culturing enables otherwise selfish people all over the planet to check outside of themselves and adjust their behaviour to fit in with and belong to something bigger and of equal interest and relevance in their lives — culture.

Culturing is what enables an individual worker to switch from being absorbed in their own thoughts, daydreams and music on the commute to work to suddenly smile or adopt a game face once they cross the threshold of their workplace. Culturing subtly demands all of us to surrender ourselves to something bigger than us — something that serves others as much as ourselves. And we are happy to do so, as the reward of contributing to a culture is that the culture contributes back to us collectively and as individuals. Because culture is what changes a person into a people it is the social glue that enables team work or company loyalty. Culturing is a powerful social phenomenon. Understand it and inspire it, and it will become a source of incredible human energy. Whenever you have seen human beings at their best or worst, you will have seen culture turning a person into a people. Culture deserves our respect in organisations because, while we are busy planning the *what* we are here to do and *who* we are here to serve, and *how* we are going to get things done, culture is determining *why* a person should join you in your endeavours and bring culture's enormous power to aid you in your efforts.

How culturing turns a person into a people will be discussed in future chapters, but for now all we need concern ourselves with is the obvious truth that it does. For people who are already able to see the wheelbarrow of culture at work in their organisation, the observation that a culture is what turns a person into a people will seem self-evident. For those still growing used to the idea that the wheelbarrow is in fact considerably more than just a wheelbarrow, my suggestion is to just keep reading.

The more you begin to understand and see culturing and how it works, the more you will become familiar and comfortable with the power that culture wields. You will also not see this power as a threat or a challenge to your business, but as a unique gift to your business—one that, if handled and led effectively, will give you a competitive advantage that others will never be able to replicate. One that your customers will compliment you on as being the essence of why they do business with you. For they too will want to connect with your culture, turning even your customers into willing and participating members of your culture. People want to belong to something that is meaningful and a positive contributor into their lives. Get your culture right and that is exactly what it will do for you, your employees, your customers, shareholders and suppliers. Why is culture so addictive and influential to billions of people around the world? Because culture is social currency.

Once you have come to understand your culture you will be in a position to see to what extent it is supporting your journey from your current results to the business results you would like to achieve in the future. If your culture is clearly defined, powerful and aligned to your business objectives, you might like to think of the culture as being like bedrock that provides a solid platform on which the organisation's performance can deliver the desired results. A culture like this is strong and reinforces itself through depth of understanding built on well-formed and -established beliefs and shared values.

However, not all organisational cultures are this strong. Especially as a result of recent years of challenging financial times, many organisations are more likely to describe their culture not as bedrock but as a battered road that has many potholes where the impact of competition and economic challenges has chipped large holes into the culture. A few organisations might recognise that the once-smooth surface of their culture has been worn out through wear and tear and now the sharp gravel underlay has been exposed, making it as painful working in the culture as it is to walk barefoot across such a stone-strewn road.

Some organisations might even suggest that the current status of their culture is more like quicksand, in that it seems to pull everything down with it. Performance is down; morale is down; customer satisfaction is down; and share prices are down.

Understanding how to build a culture that rises above these types of cultural limitations is our next step, and to achieve this we will now venture into the very heart of this book by exploring above and below the line cultures.

CHAPTER 2

Why organisations should take culture seriously

If you are new to the conversation and consideration of culture as a key contributing factor to an organisation's performance, you might be wondering if something as intangible as culture could really be that influential and, if so, why?

The short answer is 'yes': culturing always has a significant impact and influence on an organisation's performance. To answer the question 'Why?', we must consider a number of reasons, all of which deserve individual consideration. Of course you may already be a culturing convert, and already a champion inside your organisation for the recognition and development of a culture that can contribute to improved performance, customer experience and employee satisfaction. If this is the case, you might find the following familiar and yet still worthy of your deeper consideration to support you in your ongoing efforts to remind and encourage your colleagues to never let down your collective endeavours to create a high-performance culture. So why is culture worthy of being taken seriously by organisations?

The relationship of culture to business strategy

John Lennon famously wrote, 'Life is what happens to you while you're busy making other plans.' My observation is that an organisation's culture is what happens while executives are busy creating and executing 'strategic plans'. Every company that has more than two people working in it has a culture, whether those people are aware of the culture or not.

Company culture forms and develops regardless of the organisation's specific methods and systems of doing business. So while a company is busy designing or implementing a strategy, culture is already affecting that plan, in a multitude of ways. If we imagine for a moment that culture is rather like a collective mindset, then we can quickly begin to see how culture could influence even the formulating of the strategy itself. For example, the culture of the team responsible for forming the strategy will approach their task with either shared or differing opinions of what is possible. *What* defines risk. For example, which time frames for the various projects under consideration are considered too long or too short, reasonable or ridiculous? The culture of the organisation may be pessimistic or risk averse by nature, in which case the strategy may take on a noticeably conservative nature. Equally, the opposite might be true: a culture that is optimistic, future-oriented and more comfortable with risk is more able to comfortably adopt a bold strategy.

After a strategy has been formulated, agreed upon and initiated, the organisation's wider culture will have an impact on the willingness of people within the organisation to engage with and actually deliver the strategy. At this point culture's powerful influence really kicks in and affects culture in a variety of ways. Just think for a moment about how important you consider the following factors to be in terms of enabling an organisation to effectively deliver its business strategy:

- the collective attitudes, beliefs and commitment or buy-in of people in the organisation towards the strategy

- people's willingness to collaborate with one another to deliver the strategy

- the impact of inter-department or branch silo mentality on the strategy

- cultural factors, such as people's punctuality, respect for one another, sense of entitlement and tone of communication (be it friendly, arrogant, cold or warm)

- levels of discretionary effort

- people being prepared to go above and beyond the call of duty or labour regulations where extra effort or putting additional hours on a project is required

- the ability to lift the pace of the work or the attention to detail or quality

- people's sense of humour, courage or intestinal fortitude.

Do any of these factors influence your organisation's ability to get the job done? The answer is, of course, yes. However, what may not be quite so obvious is that each of these factors, along with dozens of others we could have considered, are all aspects and deliverables of your culture, and collectively they combine to add up to a considerable force. One so powerful that research conducted by Professor Mike West at the London School of Economics suggests that an organisation's culture is, on average, eight times more influential to a company's performance than strategy alone. My 30 years of exposure to organisations' cultures and the delivery of strategy leads me to completely agree with Mike West's research. If anything, I would suggest the impact is higher than eight times! You see, strategy without culturing is powerless. Yet culturing without strategy is aimless. Fun maybe, but aimless.

Does this mean that strategy isn't important? Or that we do not need strategy at all? No, of course not. Strategy is critical to an organisation's direction and focus, its objectives and aspirations, its customer value proposition and chosen markets. What it does mean is that even the world's best-designed strategy is, and always will be, dependent on an aligned company culture to drive the strategy, to give it the necessary human energy, courage, commitment and perseverance to see the job through. Over the years I have worked with many managers struggling to grasp the concept of culturing being more influential than strategy in terms of influencing results—especially those in operational or IT roles, who seem culturally biased towards the idea that a good plan alone is enough to get the job done.

To address this, I explain specifically what the words 'culture is more influential on a company's performance than strategy alone', are alluding to. If you imagine that an organisation has over-achieved or under-achieved on the delivery of its business strategy, and you then proceeded to identify all the contributing factors that led to the over- or under-achievement, you will eventually realise that, typically, there will be eight reasons relating to how culture supported or sabotaged your efforts to be successful for every one that indicates the choice of strategy was correct. A great strategy with even a slightly misaligned company culture is doomed. The original phrase that 'culture eats strategy for breakfast' could perhaps be updated to 'culture eats strategy for breakfast, lunch, dinner, morning tea, afternoon tea and as a midnight snack'.

Culture is your organisation's first competitor

I often point out to audiences in my keynote speeches on culture that Enron was not put out of business by its competition. The competition did not provide a cheaper price that Enron couldn't compete with. Competitors did not offer breakthrough technology that left Enron lagging. They did not make smarter investments or acquire or merge with better organisations than Enron could access. Enron did not succumb to a superior competitor in the marketplace: it succumbed to its own culture! When a culture becomes misaligned with the organisation's sustainability, the culture can and perhaps should be considered to be its first competitor.

In my experience, company culture is more often than not an organisation's first point of failure. (On a more positive note, which we will explore later, it is also its first sign of forthcoming success). This remarkable situation means that, for many organisations, their own company culture is a greater threat to the organisation's performance than their strongest external competitor!

Think of all the traditional threats associated with competition to a business. For example, the competition can undercut the price of your products in the market and steal your customers; offer better service, or make your service feel dated or somehow inferior; offer faster, more profitable results; provide superior technology or a more advanced version of your product; reposition your brand through the more appealing or relevant positioning of their brand; offer warmer, closer, more genuine relationships; or more accessibility through better location, opening hours or personal attention.

Consider this: with the possible exception of the point about superior technology, your own culture can sabotage each one of these areas. Let's review some of these areas in more detail to see how.

- *Undercut the price of your products in the market.* Price is a fee charged for the delivery of value in the shape of a product or service. If your culture were to affect the customer's sense of value through slow response times, or a lack of warmth and customer service at the point of sale, or a tardy and uninterested response to a customer's question at the point of sale or as part of a complaint phone call or request for customer support, the value of the product or service is undermined. In other words it achieves the same outcome as a competitor providing the product or service at a cheaper price. It makes your offering look and feel overpriced for the value added and the experience provided. The net result is that your culture took value from the customer's experience and payment. In short, your culture acted as a competitor!

- *Steal your customers.* Okay, so your culture doesn't actually steal your customers, but just like the price example the net effect is the same. An underperforming culture will force your customers into the arms or tills of your competitors.

- *Offer better service, or make your service feel dated or somehow inferior.* Again a company culture underperforming in the field of service will drive customers to your competitors. Your customers may enjoy the convenient locality of your business and respect the quality or durability of your products, but if they also experience a lack of appreciation for bringing their business to you, or that they are not respected or thanked by your employees every time they bring you that business, this culture of disengagement is more often than not enough to drive them into the arms of your competitors.

- *Reposition your brand through the more appealing or relevant positioning of their brand.* No doubt you can at this point see where I'm going in terms of how your culture can reposition your brand. When I talk about brand I mean, of course, the customer's perception of the experience of doing business with you—in other words, the combined, overall impression the customer has of your business. I am not referring to simply your company logo or brand icon. A brand icon, even one as simple and as well known as Apple's, is not a brand. It's just a logo, or at best a promise of a certain standard and experience. What that logo conjures up in the mind and sensory memory of Apple's millions of customers around the world is the real brand. Its true essence. Brand always belongs to the customers as a summary of the experience they have of your business. When your brand and its innate promise are contradicted or even sabotaged by your company culture, your brand suffers. As your brand reputation suffers comparatively, your competitor's brand can appear to rise in the eyes of your customers—your greatest competition can come from within.

When viewed from this perspective, it's obvious that culture can do as much damage to your business as the most worthy competitor! You might think of a brand as a promise and the culture as the delivery, or non-delivery, on that promise. We could have mentioned how an organisation's culture can affect staff turnover, or losing key talent to your competitors. Or culture's impact on workplace productivity, creativity and even people's willingness to serve others as examples of the possible negative impact of culture. The important point is to recognise that your own culture can do as much damage, with greater speed and stealth, to your organisation's performance than even your best-placed or strongest competitor.

I have come to firmly believe that, if you're not taking workplace culture seriously, you can almost guarantee your company culture is your number one competitor. The inability to see the competitive aspects of your own workplace culture is one of the greatest contributors to underperformance. When viewed from this perspective, it's obvious that culture can do as much damage to your business as its greatest competitor!

Culture is another word for performance

As you read through the previous discussion of how culture, when misaligned with your organisation's sustainability, can act like a competitor, you might have also picked up on the subtle reference to culture operating as performance in your organisation. I'm not referring to the outcome of the performance, which, of course, is the results generated—the sales made, revenue generated, number of faulty products, speed to market and the like. I mean the collective human behaviour, people in action—working, talking, planning, thinking, sharing, serving, lifting, carrying—in short, the culture at work. A culture in action is a performance as much as a ballet troupe working its way through *Swan Lake* on a stage, or the New Zealand All Black Rugby team delivering its consistently dominating on-field brand of 'total rugby', or Bruce Springsteen and the E Street Band belting out a catalogue of hits are performances. Culture is performance, and when organisations understand and view it as such, they immediately awaken to the degree to which culture is crucial to achieving their all-important business results. I have found that when business leaders, who would otherwise consider company culture to be too soft, intangible and airy-fairy to be worthy of their time and effort, begin to think of and see their culture as their business performance, they suddenly get it. Often they suddenly become the most active and persistent champions of company culture and lead the way in their commitment to inspire a culture worthy of retaining their best customers and employees.

The impact of the global financial crisis

The global financial crisis, even in countries such as Australia, which have been left relatively untouched, has led to a significant investment of time, attention and energy to reduce risk within businesses and cut costs. Organisations have followed four common trends to achieve these cutbacks. These are:

- *Outsourcing*: transferring various functions of the business to outside providers who can, for reasons of size, scale or expertise, provide the same service (or better) to the organisation at a lower cost than the organisation can achieve itself. A common example is closing down internal call or customer support centres and outsourcing the service to an offshore provider.

- *Restructuring*: redesigning the structure of the organisation, which could include the shrinking or even complete closure of various branches or departments. One example is the closure of regional offices and the relocation of employees into a central office. For example, this occurred for nearly all the major banks in Australia and several in New Zealand as the banks no longer consider some geographical regions to warrant their physical presence due to the minimum amount or low profit margins associated with the banking occurring in these locations.

- *Automating*: the simple replacement of humans with technology or machinery. This could include everything from installing robots on a production line or operating automated trucks in an open-cast mine, through to providing an app or some other online service to customers to enable them to complete a service that previously would have required the support or transaction of a staff member. Online banking is a common example of this.

- *Retrenching*: a strange choice of word really. It simply means sacking people to save money on wages and salaries.

All this outsourcing, restructuring, automating and retrenching really only delivers one outcome: greater efficiency.

There are two problems associated with this. First, every one of your competitors can not only achieve the same cost saving you have, but they probably have already done so, and in some cases they may have done so even more effectively than your organisation has. Second, customers expect efficiency. If they are a business customer, they expect greater efficiency, as they have been through the same rationalisation process that you have. If the customer is a consumer then, thanks to the advent of handheld techno-wizardry, they expect efficiency as they hold enormous capability in the palm of their hand. What smart phones and tablets can achieve in terms of efficiency and access to data, knowledge, communication and creativity would have made people even as recently as the early 1990s gasp in disbelief.

Efficiency isn't enough. People expect efficiency, but what they really long for is empathy, creativity, warmth, meaning and connection. It is empathy, creativity, surprise and warmth that provide customer delight — not customer satisfaction (efficiency delivers that), but delight.

There is no better source of delight that organisations can provide their customers than an amazing company culture dedicated to putting a smile on every customer's face. Customer delight occurs in the moment. It is not pre-planned as part of a service methodology, or quality system, or customer service process. Delight is achieved through an empathetic instant and unapologetic gesture or action taken to delight the customer. It relies not so much on a step-by-step customer process, which even a trained parrot could learn to deliver, such as adding the phrase 'have a nice day' at the end of every customer interaction. Customer delight is the result of a cultural commitment. One in which every employee has the empowerment of the company to do whatever can and should be done to delight a customer. This means employees and managers must be vigilant to opportunity, looking beyond efficiency and the business systems to concentrate on the customer experience. Not the 'customer experience' as an overarching value proposition or marketing ploy, but the real customer experience occurring right now at the counter, right now online and right now in the phone conversation in the call centre. Service delight happens in the moment! Right now. It is at the discretion of and in the caring hands and voice of every employee. When a company culture is dedicated to customer delight a service transformation occurs. I was fortunate enough to be invited to support the then-new CEO of Z Energy in New Zealand, which was rebranded and transformed after Infratil Ltd (the New Zealand-based infrastructure and investment company) took over Shell Oil across the country. Mike Bennet, the

CEO, and I met on several occasions before the acquisition to discuss his ideas and commitment to workplace culture.

One of the foundation commitments Mike had in mind was to put the 'service' back into stations (petrol outlets). To do so required a culture committed to delighting the customer, because, as active as Mike is at getting out and meeting and listening to people across the business across New Zealand, he couldn't be everywhere all the time. However, Mike has a unique quality as a leader. He truly believes in and backs people to be amazing and to do their best for the customer at all times. With this in mind I suggested to Mike that what the company needed was something beyond what most organisations do when describing the culture. Most organisations describe culture as 'the way we do things around here'. But to offer customer delight you need your people to move beyond the way we do things. An above the line culture is less about 'the way we do things around here' and more about 'why we do it this way around here'. Mike, being the make-it-happen CEO he is, worked with the wonderful Huma Faruqui—his general manager of capability and organisational development—to create an inspirational and fun document that outlined why everybody at Z Energy was invited to be at their best and give their best to put the service back into service stations. Along with the business smarts that got Mike the CEO's job in the first place, this approach, which has been documented in a short booklet known as 'The Z Why', has become legendary among human resource practitioners, even those working in other organisations, across the nation. This commitment to build a culture of service and delighting customers has led to some phenomenal business performance, including Z Energy achieving its first five-year strategic goals within the first 18 months of operation. When you ask Mike what he puts their phenomenal success down to, especially in such a ridiculously competitive and price-sensitive industry, he always gives the same answer: 'Our people and culture.'

If your organisation became the single provider of empathy, warmth, creativity and delivering delight, the customer experience would shift from the routine and expected to delighted, instantly. Simple yet effective. Fast, too, if you know how to build an above the line culture to help get you there. To have a whole company culture dedicated and committed to seizing every opportunity to delight a customer is a very unusual thing. As we all know, in commerce rarity equals value. People are desperate for these experiences, and if your organisation is the one with the culture to provide them, the value you add, from the customer's perspective, increases significantly. Culture adds value, and value is valued by customers.

A final thought on this topic. After the significant disappointments people have been subjected to by organisations around the world in recent times (think everything from the Barclays Bank rate-rigging corruption that made headline news around the world in mid-2012, to the BP Deepwater oil spills in the Gulf of Mexico in 2010, to the sub-prime loans debacle that kicked off the global financial crisis in 2008, to the calls for an inquiry into the Bank of England's behaviour in February 2014) people are desperate to believe in organisations again, and to trust in people within organisations again. A high-performance workplace culture can provide just that. Imagine if your organisation's culture led the way for your industry: what would be the results in terms of customer loyalty, employee job satisfaction, brand equity and supplier commitment? Worth thinking about isn't it?

Gen Y employee expectations

Culture is the third most common reason employees give for quitting their jobs. The first, as is so often publicised in media and books, is that people quit their boss, not their job. The second most common reason is that they do not enjoy the actual work, as they find it either too challenging, and in some cases overwhelming and stressful, or they suffer from the opposite experience, and they are bored. However, a toxic or unfriendly, unproductive culture is the third most commonly shared reason for quitting a job. (Lack of promotion or growth opportunity is fourth, with money or pay coming in as the fifth most common reason for quitting.)

Members of Generation Y, born between the 1980s and the early 2000s, will switch jobs more frequently than any previous generation, as they have high expectations of what organisations should offer. Among the list of expectations is a social, fun and engaging workplace culture. Gen Y have been noted as possessing a deep desire to make the world a better place, along with a recognition that organisations and institutions will not achieve this based on old-school thinking, combined with an understanding that doing so will require building new institutions both from the inside—through the transformation of their cultures—and from outside—through the demands of the changing demographics of the marketplace.

What does all this mean for your organisation? To attract and retain the best young talent and, as importantly, have them speak positively of your organisation in their social and professional networks, your organisation's culture will need to be above average and committed to ongoing development and improvement. Anything less will not match up to what employees are hearing from their peers in other organisations, and they will not hesitate to leave.

This chapter has outlined why culture should be of importance to organisations. If you need to begin conversations in your business regarding the extent to which culture's importance is understood or even acknowledged, the following checklist might prove useful as a summary of the key areas to consider.

Why organisations should take culture seriously

In summary, there are many reasons for taking culture seriously:

- When culture is misaligned with a business strategy, it will sabotage that strategy.

- When culture is aligned with the business strategy, it will accelerate the strategy.

- Culture is, more often than not, your organisation's first point of failure, and therefore your most confronting competitor.

- Culture is, more often than not, your organisation's first point of success, and therefore your most contributing ally.

- Culture either reinforces and delivers your brand's promise, or makes a liar of that promise.

- In a world battered and bruised from the global financial crisis, culture has the opportunity to provide your organisation with a competitive advantage, if in the eyes of your customers you are seen to be more empathetic and creative in your instantaneous responses to their needs. Your competitors will have simply relied, as many organisations have done, on rationalising, outsourcing, automating and restricting expenditures to manage costs and survive. This makes them more efficient, but customers expect efficiency. What they long for is delight. A customer-focused culture delivers just that.

- Generational changes in the make-up of our workplaces have shifted the expectations of employees regarding the role of organisational culture. Gen Y expects the organisation to commit to culture and excel. Anything less and they are happy to take their talents, optimism and drive elsewhere.

- Culture is the sum of all the thousands of daily behaviours exhibited in your business. Some of these are asked for by management out of a need for compliance. Many more are not. They are the result of individual discretionary choices and efforts made by individuals hundreds of times a day that are either contributing to or sabotaging your business strategy. A strong and deliberate culture aligns all the behaviours of an organisation into a powerful and energetic contribution capable of driving your business performance beyond even the objectives outlined in your strategic plan.

In the next chapter I will outline the close link between culture and strategy and how this occurs.

CHAPTER 3

Aligning culture and strategy

Organisations regularly fail to take into consideration that their culture must be aligned to their business strategy. This may seem obvious as even simply reading the words 'align to the company strategy' immediately awakens our awareness to the importance of this point.

The relationship between culture and strategy

Occasionally I find myself working with a leadership team that, despite its combined efforts, still struggles to grasp the link between culture and strategy. This usually occurs because the leaders have little or no ability to see the wheelbarrow. There comes a point where there is no point continuing to describe the attributes and influence of culture if people do not have any direct experience of culture. In other words, discussing something they have no experience of often reinforces any existing cynicism or scepticism already existing in the minds of the leaders.

In these situations I find it useful to switch from discussing the direct link between the culture and strategy, as the leaders cannot see the connection, and instead use a simple metaphor that captures the mutually dependent relationship between the two. Over years of consulting on culture to organisations, I have tried numerous metaphors to help people to make the link between culture and strategy. The most effective metaphor is one I invented which I refer to as the opposable thumb of culture. As we all know, an opposable thumb allows the digit fingers to grasp and handle objects. It is this ability to grasp objects in this manner that is a distinguishing characteristic of all primates, including, of course, humans. If we imagine that our index finger represents the organisation's strategy, and our thumb is the equivalent of the company culture, we can begin to explore the relationship between the two in a very simple and practical manner. The index finger (strategy) points the way (see figure 3.1).

Figure 3.1: the index finger points the way

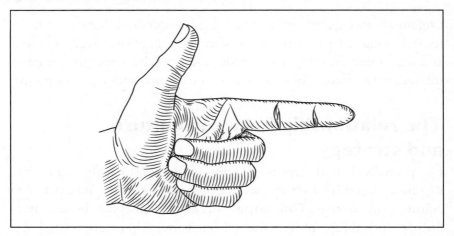

The index finger, representing strategy and the business-operation model, isolates a specific and desirable outcome or destination for the organisation. In doing so, the index finger symbolically represents the separation of one objective from the many optional goals an organisation could choose from. The thumb in this metaphor represents culture and the position of the thumb indicates whether the culture will provide its approval and willingness—thumbs up—to align to the strategic direction and outcome, or not—thumbs down (see figure 3.2).

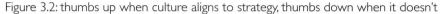

Figure 3.2: thumbs up when culture aligns to strategy, thumbs down when it doesn't

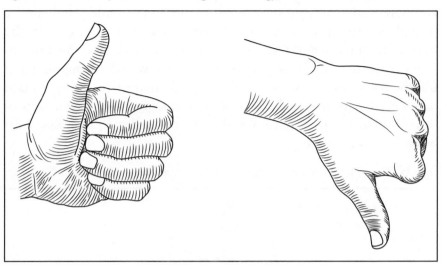

Interestingly, the thumb is the only digit on the hand that has two phalanges (bone hinges or knuckles) rather than the three found on the fingers. The two hinges can be thought of as representing either for or against. When they are for, we get a cultural thumbs up regarding the strategy, and the culture's full capability can be brought to connect with the strategy.

When the culture approves of the chosen strategy, then, and only then, can the opposable thumb (the culture) be drawn upon to close with the index finger (strategy) and grasp the opportunity to generate results (see figure 3.3, overleaf). Typically, even the most evasive manager or leader finds the opposable thumb metaphor an undeniably useful means for them to grasp the connection between culture and strategy and, more importantly, use it to explain the connection to others. It is important to ensure leaders are provided with every opportunity to enable them to see the wheelbarrow. For, as we shall see in the next chapter, although leaders do not own the organisation's culture, they do have a significant influence in terms of inspiring the culture to engage with the business in a positive and supportive relationship. The more leaders can see the power and influence of culture in shaping the organisation's performance, the more likely they will be to put the time and effort into influencing culture to align with strategy. If you have leaders in your organisation who do not understand culture or still perceive it as a soft topic, one that is best delegated to the human resource team, I strongly recommend you take the time to support them to begin to see the wheelbarrow and its ongoing and indispensable role in driving business performance. An unrecognised or ignored wheelbarrow can, as demonstrated in the Soviet factory story I shared earlier, have a real and potentially costly impact on business performance.

Figure 3.3: thumb pinched with finger creates a grasp ability

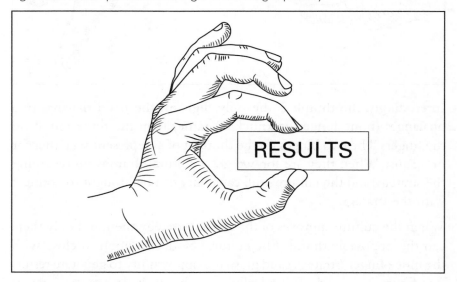

Culture and performance

At this point it might be useful to pose a question for you to consider. If you look at your organisation's current business strategy and performance, and consider this in relation to the ideal performance and results you want or need your organisation to achieve, does culture play in supporting you on this journey? Does your workplace culture have a significant role? A minor role? A moderately important role?

If you are not sure, it might be worth your while considering what you are trying to achieve strategically and then come back to the question, 'How important is our workplace culture in supporting our business to deliver on its strategic objectives?' This is an important question to consider for a number of reasons, including the following:

- The question enables you to determine why your organisation should, or should not, invest time, money, energy and effort to improve your culture. If culture has no value-contribution to make in terms of delivering a better performance or attracting good people to join your organisation to increase performance and deliver better results, then there is no need to begin culture work.

- Posing this question to your senior leadership or employees, or both, can highlight the varying perspectives held by people across your organisation as to the relative value they perceive culture can contribute to the organisation's performance and results. This can lead to important dialogue that can help you take into consideration perspectives that might otherwise have been overlooked regarding the role of culture.

- Posing this question will often highlight the extent to which people in your organisation even understand or are aware of what results are being, or need to be, generated.

- Finally, this question can also highlight how informed or aware people are of the role of culture in a business.

All four of these opportunities can provide useful insights to better inform your organisation of how to tap into further opportunities for growth and development. These are important discussions to have, as the relationship between culture and strategy is far more influential than most businesspeople give credit to. In simple terms the key question to consider can be summarised in figure 3.4 (overleaf): 'Does culture play a role in supporting our results to move from where they currently are to where we would prefer them to be?'

Figure 3.4: does culture play a role in supporting your results to move from where they currently are to where you would prefer them to be?

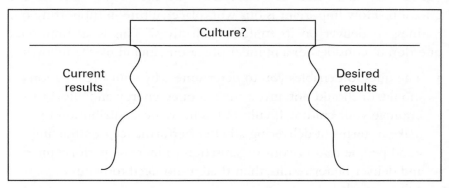

Having considered the relationship between culture and strategy, the next step is to understand how to go about aligning the two. A number of considerations have to be taken into account here. The first of which, and the focus of the next section, is to understand the importance of culture and strategy in terms of the organisation's operating models. Later in the book, we will explore other considerations such as the power of your culture, leadership, purpose and other factors.

Aligning culture and company strategy

Organisations repeatedly work on their cultures and fail to take into consideration the importance of aligning culture and strategy in creating a successful company culture. We have already discussed posing the question 'To what extent does culture play a role in supporting our organisation to move from where we are to where we want to be—from achieving our current results to achieving better results?'

Although you might readily arrive at the conclusion that your culture has a major or minor role to play in supporting you achieving your desired business results, many leaders struggle to understand or articulate anything beyond a few simple adjectives to support their argument. I have heard many leaders say things like: 'Yes we need a positive, energised culture to deliver the strategy' or 'A creative, driven culture is crucial to our success'. These two descriptions are too vague to be of any use in terms of isolating a culture that can add value to your business. Really aligning your organisation's culture to your business strategy requires you to first have absolute clarity and agreement on the strategy itself. A simple test of this is to ask your leadership team next time they gather to quickly write out a description of the current business strategy. When everyone has done so, ask them to each read out their description one by one and listen for the degree of unity the descriptions highlight. If they are aligned, great. If not? This book can help you explore how to become more aligned on your view of the culture.

Misaligned on strategy

Whenever I discover I am working with a senior leadership team that is unaligned or even confused or at odds regarding the organisation's strategy, I go back to a tried and tested strategic model that I was first introduced to when I was researching my book *Leading Through Values: Linking Company Culture to Business Strategy*. I was discussing with a client how we might link their culture more closely to their chosen strategy. To explain their chosen strategy the client referred me to the work of US business consultants Fred Wiersema and Michael Treacy, as captured in their best-selling book, *The Discipline of Market Leaders: Choose Your Customers, Narrow Your Focus, Dominate Your Market*. The book outlines some fundamental truths about the modern marketplace and customer behaviours, and how organisations can best respond to their customers' differing needs in regards to their perceptions of value. Because not every customer in the market is the same, different customers are looking for different kinds of value. As US President Abraham Lincoln said: 'You can please some of the people some of the time.' Organisations need to develop strategies to ensure they can please some of the customers all of the time. Meaning any given company can never expect to have all of the customers within a given market. However, they can work towards pleasing some of those customers repeatedly. The authors suggest that the key to success lies in narrowing the company's focus on just one key element of value. Because trying to cover all aspects of value often ends up with contradictory results. Let me explain.

Customers tend to fall into three groups, categorised by the value element they are most attracted by. The three categories of value that most businesses can tap into in order to provide for their customers are:

1 *Best product.* In this case, customers are aware of the price of your competitors' products, but are prepared to pay a premium for cutting edge design, performance and features. For example, Apple would fit into this value offering category. There are other products available at cheaper prices, but Apple's products are so elegant and easy to use that they don't even need instruction manuals.

2 *Best service.* This relates to customers who prefer to have their individual requirements understood and met through an ongoing relationship with your company. Your local family restaurant would fall into this category. Over a period of visits the waiters, chefs or owners will come to know your tastes in food and wine along with your preferred seating.

3 *Best price.* Customers who are just interested in the lowest-price reliable products that come with no-hassle delivery favour organisations delivering into this category.

Most organisations offer a mixture of all three of these value categories. They will, for example, have a product at a set price and serve customers who want to purchase the product. However, what Wiersema and Treacy are suggesting is that to excel, and in fact lead, your market in any one of these categories requires your organisation to have the discipline to choose and focus on just one of them. To try to deliver on all three becomes counterproductive, for several reasons. First, the levels of value are constantly rising. Prices become cheaper; products improve; customer service standards lift. To excel and compete on all three fronts is too demanding, especially as customer expectations in relation to all three categories are constantly rising, too. An organisation can only stay ahead of the competition if it consistently delivers more added value. Second, to invest in product development costs money, which, when invested, is a cost that at some stage will have to be covered within the pricing of the product. Aiming for top products, therefore, contradicts the cost-saving business discipline required of a price-centred value category. Likewise offering a high level of customer service requires higher skill levels, the cost of which also needs to be covered in the price, again contradicting the cost-saving business model. Each value category your organisation chooses to take on as its competitive advantage to differentiate itself in the marketplace requires a dedicated and disciplined focus and must be placed ahead of the other two disciplines in terms of investment decisions, structure and relevant culture.

Price, service or product? Pick one!

Many of my clients' leadership teams struggle to determine which of these three disciplines is or should be their priority. Many cannot even cope with the idea of prioritising one over the other two. The habit of thinking in traditional business is heavily dependent on the ability to think in strictly binary terms. Yes or no. Profitable or unprofitable. Invest or not. Retain or sack people. Buy or sell, and so on. When asked to rank the three optional value propositions, it is as if their minds cannot grasp the idea and they regularly protest, 'But they are all important.'

To help leaders come to grips with this idea, I have devised a simple yet effective model. I ask leaders to consider the three strategic disciplines as being represented by the three wheels of a tricycle (see figure 3.5, overleaf). The front wheel of your tricycle? As we all know, the front wheel is the largest and is the wheel that is connected to the handlebars and, therefore, the steering column. So the primary value discipline can be considered to be the tricycle's front wheel. As it is the largest, we also want the majority of people in the organisation to dedicate their focus and energy to it. It also, as the front wheel guides the very direction of the organisation as a whole, ensures that all decisions made within the organisation contribute in some way to ensuring the front wheel's direction is maintained.

Figure 3.5: the tricycle model

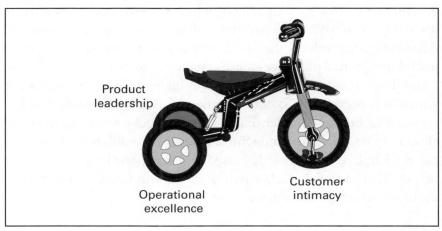

Product
leadership

Operational
excellence

Customer
intimacy

The benefit of using the tricycle model is that even those leaders from departments associated with one of the back two wheels instantly recognise that, without their contribution, the front wheel could not be projected forward to achieve its objective of delivering value to the customer. The smaller, back two wheels are seen by all as both the stabilisers for performance and the supporting energy drive.

The ability to deliver sustained value to customers requires this understanding of a separate yet ultimately supportive mixture of disciplines, with one chosen as the front runner or front wheel.

From customer value to operating model

Having chosen its front wheel of customer-adding value, the organisation must then align its operating model with this objective in a variety of ways. The organisation's operating model will be a mixture of the structure, management system, operating systems, finance model and culture, which are all focused on delivering customer value. Each of the value categories of price, service and product requires a different operating model. Again, Wiersema and Treacy's research insists that, in order to deliver outstanding levels of value in one area, organisations must commit to one of the following operating models. Failure to do so leads to split attention and focus and contradictory operational functions and objectives leading to mediocre performance and customer experiences.

The following discussion provides brief outlines of these operating models and I strongly recommend you read Wiersema and Treacy's book, *The Discipline of Market Leaders*.

Customer intimacy

Organisations that deliver value through customer intimacy are committed to building long and deep relationships with their customers. In this model, the organisation's focus is to always deliver exactly what the individual customer wants. Think of a waitress at a breakfast asking you how you would like your eggs, and no matter what you say, the waitress will instruct the chef to deliver exactly that. You know you have walked into an organisation that doesn't do customer intimacy when you ask for a boiled egg and the waitress tells you they only do poached or scrambled. Responding to such individual customer needs is called 'tailoring' in Wiersema and Treacy's book. The main features of this type of organisational operating model are:

- a company culture that encourages always going the extra mile for clients

- business systems that focus on and reward a small number of select clients

- an organisation that ensures all service offerings encourage a long-term relationship with the client

- a company that empowers employees (within reason) to make any decisions on the spot that will delight the customer.

Operational excellence

An organisation attempting to deliver the mix of value offered through quality, price and ease of purchase better than anyone else will focus on operational excellence, in other words, execution. The main features of this type of organisational operating model are:

- streamlined processes standardised to minimise costs and problems
- usually a low tolerance for mistakes: failure is not an option
- tight control of all procedures and logistics: significant decisions are made by leadership and management, never staff
- management systems focused on efficiency and consistency
- a company culture that rewards efficiency and consistency.

Product leadership

An organisation committed to excelling at adding value through their products will continually add new features and benefits to the products or update the product with a 2.0 offering. Being the first to launch a new product range is another key focus of this operating model. The main features of this type of organisational operating model are:

- a company culture that encourages ideation and the ongoing advancement of counterintuitive or evolutionary thinking
- failure is an option as it is seen as a learning experience; however, failing fast and early is preferred
- invention and innovation are ongoing—research and development budgets in these organisations are always substantial
- less reliance on functional roles and more on a matrix model or project teams that dissolve when the project's objectives are achieved.

Having considered the three customer value options and their correlating operational models, let's just pause for a moment and review what we have learnt so far. Figure 3.6 highlights the key components.

Figure 3.6: does culture influence your strategy?

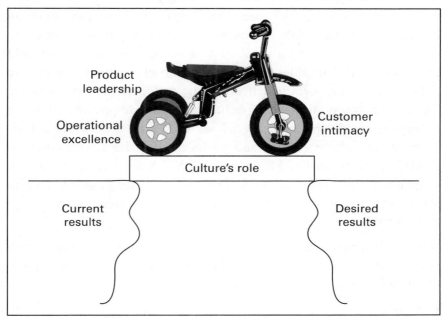

We have now added to the original concept of an organisation determining what results are desired for the future, and to what extent the company culture will play a role in advancing towards these objectives, by adding the idea that one of the three strategies and supportive operating models should be chosen in order to ensure maximum alignment of the organisation's processes and systems.

Just clarifying this one strategic discipline alone can significantly enhance an organisation's ability to perform and transition from its current results to its desired results. In other words we can now see we are deliberately moving from the current results to the desired results by disciplining our decisions, investments and activities through our chosen front-wheel operating model to achieve our desired results, delivered through achieving everything we possibly can relating to our chosen customer value proposition.

Values alignment to strategy

As we saw in each of the three brief explorations of the operating models, culture has a role to play in supporting the delivery of every customer value proposition. We will now go one step further and identify the cultural values groups that enable an organisational culture to best align to support the delivery of the customer value proposition. To support your understanding of how a culture can possibly influence an organisation's operating model we must first understand a little more about culture. Author and professor of management emeritus at MIT Sloan School of Management Edgar Schein, in his book *The Corporate Culture Survival Guide*, provides a beautiful, simple and, in my experience, accurate model for understanding how cultures form and operate.

Schein suggests there are three distinct layers to culture worth considering. On the first, or surface, level culture consists of the observable and audible elements, such as:

- artefacts
- icons
- people's behaviours
- furnishing
- language and conversations
- jingles, music, anthems
- symbols and icons.

The second layer of culture consists of the underlying and unseen motivational aspects known as the layer of human values. The third and deepest layer relates to the underlying assumptions and transparent belief systems, often referred to as the unwritten ground rules of a culture.

The second layer of values in this three-tier conception of culture is an area I have specialised in for many years.

I used a comprehensive values inventory, administered and developed by Paul Chippendale, of the Minessence Values Education Centre, which includes the 128 known human values. I worked with Paul to identify three groups of values that I suspected each of the three operating models would be reliant upon if they wanted to have the people delivering, overseeing and managing the systems to stay focused and diligently dedicated to the systems. If you are interested in the somewhat logical leap that led to the consideration that the 128 human values might relate to the delivery of the three strategic disciplines of operational excellence, product leadership and customer intimacy, you might refer to the book I wrote with my practice partners on the subject called *Leading Through Values*.

The work Paul and I undertook led to the discovery that the 128 human values fall into three distinct categories. First, we identified a group of values that were to do with having a motivation to experience control in life. The second group were values to do with people's motivation for relating to other people. The last group was a set of values that motivated people to grow and develop themselves or the systems and processes humans use to engage in the world. Not surprisingly, we named these three categories of values control, relating and development. Since discovering these three sets of values I have reviewed all my work and field notes as an anthropologist and also observed that at every organisation I come into contact with (as a consultant or as a customer), I have consistently found these three groups of values to be present in all cultures. A simple and useful exercise you can conduct is next time you are at work, pay attention to what people are doing and then consider what are the underlying motivations for the action, behaviour or conversation you are witnessing. I suspect you will that find all human activity you witness will be an attempt to *control something, relate to somebody* or *develop a pathway, insight, knowledge, solution or answer.*

I have provided a sample of some of the 128 values from each group here to help you gain a sense of the type of values that motivate people in terms of controlling, relating and developing. If you are not that interested in the specific values just jump ahead a few pages to the continuing dialogue. The following are the sample human values in the three categories.

I. The relational values examples: relating

- *Accountability/ethics*—to hold yourself and others accountable to a code of ethics derived from your values. To address the appropriateness of your behaviour in relation to your values.

- *Accountability/rule*—to be held accountable to established rules, codes of conduct, procedures, standards, and so on.

- *Collaboration*—to work cooperatively with a common purpose, sharing responsibility and accountability.

- *Communal discernment*—to elicit communal wisdom in order to determine appropriate actions through careful reflection, and honest, open dialogue.

- *Congruence*—to align one's words, actions and deeds with espoused beliefs. (Walk the talk. Practice what you preach.)

- *Empathy*—to deeply relate with others in such a way that they feel understood.

- *Family/belonging*—to have a place or sense of home; to be devoted to people you consider family and to experience belonging and acceptance.

- *Generosity*—to unconditionally share your resources, talents and skills as a way of serving others.

- *Hospitality/courtesy*—to treat others, and be treated by them, in a polite, respectful, friendly and hospitable manner.

- *Human dignity*—to observe the basic right of every human being to have respect and to have their basic needs met in a way that will allow them the opportunity to develop their potential.

- *Loyalty*—to strictly observe promises and duties to those in authority and to those in close personal relationships.

- *Presence/being*—to be there for another person in such a way that increases their self-knowledge and awareness.

- *Sharing/listening/trust*—to actively and accurately hear and sense another's thoughts and feelings. To express your own thoughts and feelings in a climate of mutual trust.

2. The control values examples: controlling

- *Administration/control*—to exercise administrative and/or management functions and tasks.

- *Communication/information*—to ensure the effective and efficient flow of ideas and factual information.

- *Control/order/discipline*—to maintain control and order through rules and discipline.

- *Duty*—to follow customs, regulations and institutional codes out of a sense of duty.

- *Efficiency/planning*—to plan systems and activities that will maximise the use of available resources.

- *Financial security*—to accumulate financial wealth in order to be secure.

- *Financial success*—to achieve financial success through the effective and efficient control and management of resources.

- *Hierarchy/protocol*—to have a methodical arrangement of persons and things, ranked above one another, in conformity with established standards of what is good and proper within an organisation.

- *Law/rule*—to live life by the rules—to govern your conduct, action and procedures by the established legal system.

- *Management*—to control and direct people in order to achieve optimal productivity and efficiency.

- *Membership/organisation*—to take pride in belonging to and having a role in any form of organisation.

- *Obedience*—dutiful compliance with moral and legal obligations established by authorities.

- *Productivity*—to be energised by generating and completing tasks and activities, and be keen to meet or exceed set goals and expectations.

- *Rationality*—to think formally, logically and analytically, preferring reason to emotion.

- *Unity/control*—establishing and maintaining efficiency, order, loyalty and conformity to established norms.

- *Work*—to have the skills, confidence and desire to engage in productive work.

3. Development values examples: developing

- *Achievement*—to accomplish something noteworthy and admirable in your work, education or your life in general.

- *Adaptability/flexibility*—to be flexible and adaptable in response to changing circumstances.

- *Construction/new order*—to initiate and develop a new form of organisation.

- *Convivial technology*—to apply technology for the benefit of humanity and the planet.

- *Creative ideation*—to transform ideas and images into concrete form.

- *Decision/initiation*—to take personal responsibility for setting direction and initiating action.

- *Discovery and insight*—to be motivated by moments of discovery and insight.

- *Education/knowledge*—to engage in ongoing learning to gain new facts, principles and insights.

- *Faith/risk/vision*—to commit to a venture, or cause, even if it means personal risk.

- *Fantasy/play*—to seek personal worth through unrestrained imagination and personal amusement.

- *Human rights*—to create the means for every person in the world to experience their basic right to life-giving resources, such as food, habitat, employment, health and a minimal practical education.

- *Independence*—to be free to think and act for yourself, unrestricted by external constraint.

- *Leadership/new order*—leading/developing a new organisation or transforming an existing one.

- *Minessence*—to miniaturise and simplify complex ideas or technology into concrete and practical applications for the purpose of creatively enhancing society.

- *Organisational growth*—to creatively enable an organisation to change and grow.

- *Organisational mission*—to define and pursue an organisation's mission.

- *Pioneerism/progress*—to pioneer new ideas (including technology) for societal change and providing the framework for realising them.

- *Research/original knowledge*—to systematically investigate and contemplate truths and principles that lie behind our experience of reality to create and communicate original insights.

These three values sets provide the underlying motivation and meaning of a culture. Cultures usually combine all three values sets in their view of the world. However, because of the surrounding context in which a culture finds itself, usually one of these sets of values tends to dominate the other two. This occurs for two reasons. First, because one of the values sets has more values that are shared by people. The second reason can be that the shared values from one particular set are also held as being of more importance or of higher priority than values from other sets.

Cultures with an emphasis on the control values tend to do better at aligning and executing with the operational excellence operating model. Cultures with a emphasis on the relational values tend to do better at aligning and executing with the customer intimacy operating model. Cultures with an emphasis on the development values tend to do better at aligning and executing with the product leadership operating model. This makes sense, as all the things that need to be attended to in each of these distinct operating models require a different set of motivating and directional influences. In other words, they are dependent on a unique set of aligned values to guide people's behaviours, actions and decisions. Because these values are organic and therefore naturally embodied in the culture, the effort required to deliver on the values is minimal, because the effort will always feel natural to the people in this culture. It is their preferred way of operating. Their own personal values demand and guide them to behave in a way that fits perfectly into the operating model, which in turn feeds into the delivery of the customer value proposition. We can see the relationship of this natural fit in table 3.1.

Table 3.1: the relationship between values and operating models

Values set	Operating model	Customer value
Control	Operational excellence	Price
Relating	Customer intimacy	Service
Developing	Product leadership	Product

As you might expect, whenever I have come across a culture whose values preference is misaligned with their intended operating model and therefore their delivery of the desired customer value, the organisation's performance is affected. As this occurs quite regularly, I have reached the conclusion that many organisations are losing productivity and suffering lower performance simply because they have never made the link between these cultural values and their operating models.

Whenever I help organisations clarify their controlling, relating and developing values in this manner, the people in the organisation find the process incredibly illuminating, as it provides explanations of why people are behaving the way they do.

When I provide the same process focused on just clarifying the dominant values held by the leadership team, the results can be very telling. Over the years I have seen a leadership group's highest-priority shared values be so strongly drawn from one set of values that they always favoured the operating model that best aligned with their own values. For example, when I worked with a strategic planning team in a food and manufacturing plant that had dominant development values and consequently favoured the product leadership strategy. However, after sharing this bias with the team and revisiting the organisation's need for growth into new markets, they quickly realised that better and newer products were not what they needed; in fact, cheaper, faster delivery was. They were then able to use their values preference of developing to consider how they could create cheaper, faster delivery to gain access into lucrative overseas markets.

In another case, I worked with a broadcasting organisation that favoured operational excellence operating models. At the time they were trying to work out how to gain more advertising from specific clients. Because of their values bias, they constantly came up with ways to offer cheaper packages of advertising to attract additional business from clients. But whatever they offered to clients didn't seem to work. When I made them aware of their strategic bias and showed them they favoured operational excellence, it suddenly dawned on the team that maybe the customer didn't want cheaper prices at all. Maybe they wanted a closer working relationship with greater input and expertise from the broadcaster. Or maybe the clients wanted innovative advertising packages to break into new markets and not cheaper packages to continue to advertise to their established markets. Both options turned out to be popular with clients and sales boomed.

In a final example, I worked with a leadership team in an insurance organisation that was dominant in the relational values and naturally leaned towards favouring a customer intimacy strategy. Having pursued this strategic focus, they had in fact made good ground in attracting new clients and maintaining established ones too. The problem was sales had begun to plateau. On highlighting the bias they had for customer intimacy, I was able to facilitate their consideration of the other two strategic approaches to explore new opportunities. As a result of their efforts, the company developed a series of new insurance offerings and increased sales from both new and existing customers.

The point is that, just because the leadership teams combined personal and highest-priority shared values and so favoured a particular operating model did not mean that this was the best choice for the business or its customers. This type of strategic bias inevitably ends up leading to a decrease in performance and productivity.

As we learned in an earlier chapter, culture on average has eight times more impact on an organisation's performance than the chosen strategy. Which means that if the existing operating model, instead of being aligned with the leadership's personal values, was misaligned, the leadership team's culture is likely to constantly be sabotaging the strategy.

To better understand how the cultural values can have such a dramatic impact on the organisation's performance we need to understand a little more about the role and impact of human values.

Understanding values

What are values? How do they differ from morals and ethics? How do values function and what is their role in an organisation? Are they as important as many organisations say they are? How do values contribute to an organisation's performance? Each of these questions deserves some exploration to really understand the power of values and their influence inside a culture, especially in an above the line culture. Let's begin our investigation of values with the obvious question.

What are values?

There are many ways of defining values, ranging from motivation descriptions through to academic ones. After 20 years of working with and studying values, I made my definition of values short, accurate and functional. I define a human value as your 'preferences multiplied by priority, which highlights your meaning and motivation!' I recognise that this description looks a little cryptic, so let's break it down.

Values are preferences

Values can be thought of as a preference because a value is a concept. A value is not a material object or a person or a place; rather it is what these various things represent to us. What they mean to us, and not the things themselves. For example, a house is not a value, but what the house represents to us—a home, security, an investment, a status symbol—is. So a value is a preference because a value helps us identify what we would prefer to experience in our lives, by means of owning physical possessions—house, car, mobile phone, guitar; or relating to specific people, for example through friendship, romance, family, learning, support, healing, business; or engaging in specific activities such as dance, surfing, cooking, gardening, travelling, listening to music or riding a motor bike. For an organisation the preferences might be to grow, survive, compete, deliver, service, return, share or lead.

As you can imagine it doesn't take long for the preferences to become numerous. Because both individuals and organisations usually have multiple preferences it becomes important to prioritise these preferences in order to understand which are the most important, or at least important, to us.

Values as priorities

In a previous book, *Finding True North: Live Your Values, Enhance Your Life*, I wrote on personal values. I explained that in order to experience happiness and fulfilment in life, 'the most important thing is to know what is the most important thing'. The same applies to values. The most important thing to know about your values, personal or organisational, is which are the most important values. The reason is that until we have put our values into a hierarchy of importance we may find ourselves torn between conflicting values. The only way to resolve a values conflict is to understand which values are more important to you and then act accordingly! When you have a values hierarchy, you can make a clear distinction about the appropriate decision to make and then act on this with no other values in friction or resistance.

So if we work with values as our preferences multiplied by the priority we place on the individual preferences, we end up with clarity. Let me show you an example of how this might work. Imagine an individual has a preference to experience the following in their life:

- health

- family

- security

- employment
- fun
- adventure
- learning.

If they were to simply start living these values without prioritising them, they are likely to quickly find some of the values in conflict with one another. For example, being employed may reduce the amount of time they get to spend with their family and, due to the stress they might experience at work, jeopardise their health. Or they may find that pursuing their desire for adventure puts their value of health, family and security at risk. However if the person is able to do the necessary deeper contemplation and understand their prioritisation of these values, suddenly the most important things are clearly understood as the most important things and so the individual can think, plan and act accordingly without feeling guilty or stressed about their choices, as they already know what is most important to them. So let's say the person prioritises their values in the following manner:

- family
- health
- security
- fun
- learning
- employment
- adventure.

Now the individual has a clear sense of where to put their attention, time, money, energy and quality. With family defined as the value that is most important, then even having less time for adventure becomes an acceptable trade-off as the individual has made a clear decision and commitment to invest themselves in family first. Does this mean they never get to indulge their passion for adventure? No, of course not. What it does mean is that they will happily scale the quest for adventure to fit into their higher priority for family. It also means they look for different ways of experiencing adventure, perhaps in ways that include rather than exclude family participation, or in ways that only take a few hours at the weekend rather than a whole weekend away from family.

An organisation's official values may be set by the same process. Let's imagine an organisation has this set of values:

- integrity
- respect
- customer service
- growth
- innovation.

Without having a sense of hierarchy applied to the values, we can again immediately see how some of these values could end up in conflict with one another. For example, if the organisation puts time, money, people and energy into growth and innovation, it might reduce the necessary dedication and focus required to deliver on customer service, which would mean the organisation was out of integrity, claiming to be committed to service but then taking its eye off the service ball. That's not to say any organisation investing in growth and or innovation will therefore drop its standards in service, but it could, and organisations often do! However if the values are prioritised, we might end up with the values listed like this:

- customer service
- integrity
- respect
- innovation
- growth.

Suddenly we have a clear mandate for prioritisation of decision making across the organisation. Growth and innovation, for example, will still be applicable and executed, as long as these priorities have no detrimental impact on customer service.

All of this exploration and explanation of preferences multiplied by priority bring us to the final part of the equation, which is meaning and motivation. In short, once values are placed in a hierarchical order and understood, then people can grasp the meaning embodied in the values—for example always put family, or customer service first—and will be motivated to act accordingly.

Having defined values, let's now move onto the next question in our list.

How do values differ from morals and ethics?

Values are about preferences and priorities. Morals are a perspective of what is right or wrong, good or evil. Ethics are a group's agreed-upon code of behaviour.

Values, morals and ethics can be interlinked. For example, considering our previous hierarchy of values in a company, if we value customer service as our highest-priority value, then we would consider it to be wrong to treat a customer badly, or rudely. In order to ensure no employee did so, the organisation might draw up a list of behavioural guidelines that they ask everyone to abide by. Things such as always be polite in your tone, words and behaviour; always listen and ask questions before responding to the customer's needs; and be empathetic, and try to put yourself in the customer's shoes.

Although values, morals and ethics do often interlink, they also have significantly different definitions and roles.

How do values function?

Values are incredibly influential on people's performance and behaviours. By exploring some of the ways that values influence us we can begin to see how they play such a large role in determining our behaviours and performance. Our values can influence us in many ways.

Values direct our attention

Our personal values operate in very much the same way that an internet search word does. Values enable the brain to focus our attention onto a singular topic. Imagine you wanted to hire a speaker for your next conference to come and talk to the leadership team or staff about the importance of culture to organisational performance and staff fulfilment. You might open an internet search window and type in the words 'company culture expert'. The moment you hit the enter button on your keyboard you will be presented with a list of sources and options regarding speakers for your conference. The search word you typed in enables the internet search engine to isolate from the whole of the world wide web the options that are most closely aligned with your search interest.

Your personal values act in exactly the same way: they inform the reticular activated system in your brain, which maintains consciousness and acts as a filter, which in turn enables us to concentrate on what is most important to us and ignore everything else. Knowing which are your highest-priority values enables you to focus effectively on accessing and experiencing what you want, without being led astray or distracted by less important ideas, activities or topics. It is very important for people to know their personal values to ensure they are aligned with the type of work they are engaged in. People with values that are aligned with the work they do are more focused and productive, and more emotionally and mentally rewarded by their work. People who have minimal alignment between their values and the work they are engaged in have the following common symptoms. They are:

- less focused
- less productive
- more prone to mistakes
- more prone to absenteeism
- more likely to quit their jobs
- more inclined to suffer from boredom
- more likely to badmouth the work environment when talking with colleagues.

Values generate motivation

As we discovered earlier in this book, all human values fall into three broad categories of motivation: controlling, relating or developing. This means that an individual's personal values, regardless of their position in the organisation, influence the way in which they choose to relate to other people in the organisation, colleagues and customers alike; how they pay attention to ensuring and maintaining an element of control around such topics as productivity, safety, management, quality and the like; and to what extent and in what manner they see the need for their own or the organisation's growth, learning, development or improvement. The combination of focus, attention and importance on controlling, relating and developing is unique to each individual and influences directly why and how they do anything!

Values generate energy

If you have ever found yourself so involved in a piece of work, conversation, task, book, movie or song that you felt energised just by being attentive, you have felt your values at work. When you are engaged in an activity that is closely aligned with your values, you will have felt no sense of time, no need for sustaining food or drink — or if you did it felt like an interruption, something to be achieved as quickly as possible so you could get back to what you were doing. Alternatively, you will have noticed that when an activity was not aligned with your values, time dragged, your energy levels dropped, you needed all sorts of sustenance or energy-providing resources to keep you going. Why the difference? Values that are aligned to an activity generate energy. Values misaligned to an activity drain energy.

Values define what to say yes and no to

Given our values are as we discovered earlier in the discussion of our preferences and priorities, they lead to us voicing our opinion in terms of yes or no, depending on whether the question being considered aligns with our highest priority values or not. If something aligns with our values we will say yes.

Values define what is worth striving for

Our personal values define if we will embrace the company values, and if we are willing to strive for our goals or the organisation's objectives. I constantly remind people in organisations that the real power of the company culture comes from their personal values. Organisational values only become effective when people in the organisation can align their personal values with them. Otherwise the personal values will remain the dominant factor in determining people's behaviours.

The role of values in an organisation

All values have one of two distinct roles. They are either a *goal value* or a *means value*. A goal value is a value that is an end objective — the end result or outcome we are aiming for. A means value is any value that provides a way of achieving the goal value. A means value is the means to achieving the goal. If a goal value is profit, a means value for profit would be productivity, efficiency or management. Most goal values have multiple means values.

Within an organisation we can also look at the company values as goal values. The employees' personal values, when aligned with their work and the organisation, are the means values. In other words, through people delivering on and through their own personal values that are aligned with the work they are engaged in, they deliver a performance that takes the organisation towards the company goals. This is an aspect of values alignment that is little understood by organisations, and yet it directly affects performance. Organisations that clarify and define their company values, but do no work on supporting employees to identify and align their personal values to their work and the company values, are probably wasting their time. Personal values have significantly more impact on employees' levels of commitment and motivation to excel through and with their work than the organisation's values.

Research by Kouz and Pousner, two academics from Santa Clara University in the United States and authors of the book *The Leadership Challenge*, has shown that people's understanding of the organisational values makes little difference to their levels of commitment to their work compared with people clarifying their own personal values and the degree of alignment these values have to the work they do. It is only when people's personal values align with and do not contradict company values that the latter will be embodied in people's decisions and behaviour. In this manner we can begin to see how people's personal values are the *means* to the organisation's *goal* values being delivered. Finally, people who share similar or even the same values and give them similar priorities are likely to get on well. So well, that they will form and build a culture around and upon those shared high-priority values.

Are values as important as organisations think they are?

Having reviewed the role of values, we can see that they are very important to organisational culture and performance. People who believe that values are soft or touchy-feely do so out of naivety. Any half-sensible businessperson who understands even half of what values do and how they function will see the power and influence they have over performance. Without values, nothing happens. Values are the invisible threads behind so much of what organisations take for granted or are interested in achieving. Here is a short list of some of the most common ways in which values contribute to an organisation's results and performance:

- Values determine why customers choose you and your products and services.

- Values determine why people choose to join and leave your organisation.

- Values determine how much discretionary effort people will put into their work.

- Values determine whether people enjoy working with their colleagues or respect their superiors.

- Values determine whether shareholders will buy your shares.

- Values are at play in determining whether the merger or acquisition of your organisation with another, or theirs with yours, will be effective.

- Values are the underlying influence on every one of the thousands of decisions and behaviours that are made across your organisation every day.

- Values determine people's buy-in to the company culture, vision, mission and strategy.

- Values even influence which strategy the leadership team selects.

- Values determine whether your people will get along with each other.

- Values are people's means to living their organisation's goal values.

- Values are the evaluation filters that every goal and objective is subconsciously tested against by everyone. If the goals and objectives are not aligned with the values, the values win. Every time. No exception.

Having had an in-depth look at the roles of values in organisations, we are now ready to extend our focus and thinking to the wider context in which all human values function. That context is of course culture, which can occur in two dominant forms, which I refer to as above and below the line.

Part II

ABOVE THE LINE CULTURE

EXCELLING

SUCCESSFUL

STABLE

DYING

DEAD

CHAPTER 4

Above and below the line cultures

In chapter 3 we began to make the link between an organisation's current results, its desired results and the role of culture in supporting the journey from one to the other. We explored how strategy and operating models are directly affected by the three human values sets of controlling, relating and developing. Having deepened our understanding of cultures at work in chapter 1, we are now ready to progress further into the model of this book, creating an above the line culture.

Albert Einstein once commented that we cannot truly claim to understand something until we can explain it or present it as a metaphor. The latest research from neurobiologists seems to reinforce this idea—even going as far to say that we need metaphors to truly express ideas so that others can relate to them. Many different metaphors are used to understand and describe organisations. Gareth Morgan, distinguished research professor at York University in Toronto, Canada, wrote a wonderful book, *Images of Organisation*, which highlights eight of the more common metaphors used to understand and think about organisations. They described the organisation as:

- a political system
- a system of flux and change
- a culture

- an organism
- a brain
- a machine
- a psychic prison
- an instrument of domination.

In Australasia I have found that the most common metaphors used by organisations to understand themselves are:

- an instrument of domination (the organisation is a military unit)
- a machine
- a system of flux and change.

In most cases, the best way of determining the dominant metaphor organisations have adopted to describe themselves is to listen closely to the language people throughout the organisation use to discuss day-to-day business and the challenges they face. I believe all eight of Morgan's metaphors are as much a language as they are a metaphor. Think of some of the language associated with each of the three most common metaphors:

- an instrument of domination (military unit): attack the market, defend our position, launch a new product, the troops at the front line, a barrage of information, create a beach head, acquisition, beat the competitors
- a machine: grease the wheels, change gears, gear up, step into over-drive, realign ourselves, reduce friction, accelerate, steer our way through this
- a system of flux and change: adapt, manage, respond, proactive, reactive, change management, mission, vision, restructure, merge, risk management.

I have written extensively and delivered hundreds of keynotes comparing organisations to traditional tribes and, in doing so, fallen into Morgan's metaphor of seeing and thinking about organisations as a culture. I have done so for several reasons. First, I have been trained as an anthropologist. Second, I believe that, although we tend to think of modern organisations as sophisticated and smart, filled with the latest MBA thinking and with access to world-leading technology, in many respects they really do resemble a traditional culture or tribe. Modern organisations can be seen to have their equivalent. Consider these examples:

- Chief = CEO
- Hunter and gatherer = sales and marketing
- Tribal drummer = information technology/communication officer
- Shaman = chief financial officer
- Medicine man and woman = human resources
- Warriors = sales representatives
- Tribal councillors or elders = board of directors

The metaphor of a modern organisation as a tribe is still proving useful, especially for employees who are desperate to find a way of owning and working with the culture in a real-time, human way, as opposed to having it interpreted for them through climate or engagement surveys and methodologies that typically separate the people within the culture from the culture itself.

Discovering above and below the line cultures

In this book I have chosen to play with another metaphor. I have described culture as a choice, one in which people within organisations choose, either deliberately or accidentally, to create a culture that is above or below a specific line. This line can be thought of as a border or crossing point defining where a culture sits. An above the line culture is a fulfilling one in which to work, and effective in delivering results. Such a culture empowers people to progress and serve others. A below the line culture is an unpleasant one to work in, as it is stressful and feels socially unsafe. It is largely unproductive and one that succumbs to the worst of human behaviour—a culture that is driven by by fear and fosters antisocial and defensive behaviours that lead to poor performance.

In this chapter I will describe the key characteristics of cultures when they are above or below the line. I have identified these characteristics over a 25-year period of watching and listening to workplace and traditional cultures around the world. Let's start with the typical traits a culture will demonstrate when operating below the line.

Below the line culture traits

The common characteristics of cultures or people in the cultures that have fallen below the line are:

- misaligned to strategy
- fearful
- angry
- taking
- draining
- empty
- lost
- disingenuous
- sense of rumour
- adopting silo mentality
- attention turned in
- childish
- reactive
- blame storms
- pessimistic
- high staff turnover.

Misaligned to strategy

The first trait is an obvious one given what we have learned so far about the relationship between culture and strategy. A below the line culture works against the business strategy. Sometimes this is deliberate.

Often it is through unconscious incompetence. The reasons for a culture becoming misaligned with strategy will become clear as you read through the following traits, starting with the next one which, without question, has a crippling effect on organisations.

Fearful

The fundamental characteristic of a culture that has fallen below the line is that it is filled with fear. Some people talk of fear as being a useful motivating factor, and it can be. However, in cultural and below the line terms, I am referring to the more negative aspects of fear. I'm talking about fear that makes people afraid of turning up for work because they are worried about being bullied by their boss or colleagues. Or they are afraid of being made redundant through no fault of their own as the organisation goes through yet another round of restructuring. Or they are fearful of missing their deadlines or targets or sales objectives, and losing out on their bonus or being invited onto the next project team. People are afraid of the future, of making mistakes, of missing out, of not being kept informed and of unhappy customers. Fearful cultures are toxic and end up with people feeling hurt, battered and emotionally scarred. A key symptom of a culture that is in the grip of fear is anger.

Angry

Any psychologist will tell you that anger is an emotional cover or expression of an underlying fear or stress, which isn't necessarily so much an expression of fear as it is of frustration. Anger, and more specifically angry people, seem to become very common in a culture that has dropped below the line. The bosses are angry with the board and the employees. The employees are angry with each other, and angry with the bosses and the customers. Often the anger is disguised so as not to be too blatant, and shows up as sarcasm and cynicism.

Taking

All sorts of taking occurs in below the line cultures. Some of the most common forms of taking are taking credit for something you should not. For example, a salesperson might take credit for a sale, when in fact it was a customer service representative that recommended the product to the customer in the first place. Another common form of taking is when we take other people for granted. We have all seen this happen where a person takes their colleague's help for granted and forgets to say thanks. Or a manager takes for granted the team's additional input of time and energy to complete a project on time and fails to acknowledge or recognise their contributions. Perhaps the worst example is when someone in the organisation takes the customer's business for granted and fails to express appreciation for their custom.

The most common form of taking is using company time to achieve personal tasks. I have seen every version imaginable of this form of taking, including using company time for personal shopping, or playing computer games, or completing personal online banking. Taking can also occur in an emotional context, when for example people steal others' confidence, morale and optimism. Taking can of course consist of straight-out theft. This can include stealing company property, such as stationery and technology, or taking liberties with company credit cards, or taking the intellectual property of the company and selling it to another organisation. No matter what form of taking occurs, it is always an indication that your culture is below the line.

Draining

Below the line cultures are draining, tiring and exhausting. Below the line cultures do not feel safe for the people who work within them. When I say safe, I mean socially safe. In other words, people do not trust one another or feel that their comments or shared thoughts and ideas will be kept as secrets or handled discreetly. Below the line cultures are exhausting to work in as they lack group synergy and effective teamwork or cohesion. This is because the social fabric of the group has been undermined through backstabbing, lying and taking and withholding information and resources. Getting anything done in a below the line culture is harder work that it need be. In these cultures, people arrive at work dreading the day, knowing they will go home with no energy left to share with their family. In fact, they are going to have to spend the evening relaxing or recuperating enough just so they have enough strength to go back into work tomorrow and do it all again. The pace people are required to work at, the negativity of colleagues, the stress placed upon them by a demanding boss, customers and suppliers sucks every kilowatt of energy out of them and they find they don't even seem to have enough time at lunch to rest, recharge and eat.

Empty

People feel empty in a below the line culture: empty of energy, meaning, fun, joy, friendliness, values, hope, purpose, possibility and vision. Why is this? Because a below the line culture tends to be filled with egotistically driven behaviours. Everyone is out for themselves: although this can and does lead to people achieving desired results for themselves, these achievements too often feel hollow and empty. Friendships are hard to make and maintain in a culture below the line as everyone is watching out for themselves. They have learned that if they don't look out for number one nobody else will. The result is people feel isolated from one another and, as human beings are social animals, we sense deep within ourselves that this is not right: this is not what we want for ourselves or others. When we fail to socialise or connect with one another, we lose opportunities for shared fun and humour. The net result of this isolation is that people feel empty inside themselves, as if the culture has somehow become a vampire and sucked out their very life.

Lost

People feel lost inside a below the line culture. They forget what the work is for, or overlook the work's ultimate purpose of serving customers or solving client problems. They have lost the sense or understanding of what the work is really all about, other than making shareholders rich — shareholders they have never met in person and don't care about. Or they have become separated from their customers through the use of technology or automation, so employees feel disconnected from the very people who benefit from their labour. They have lost the high-touch nature of their work in which they interacted daily with real human beings, be they customers or colleagues, and find themselves having to rely on technology to achieve the same result. The work becomes just a never-ending list of tasks

People lose a sense of who they really are in a below the line culture. They forget they are creative, talented, emotional human beings and slowly dissolve to become ghosts in the machine, having lost their drive, ambitions, hopes and aspirations.

Disingenuous

In below the line cultures people speak of losing a sense of authenticity: everyone seems disingenuous or insincere. The boss doesn't really care about the workers or the customers, she only seems to care about her boss. Colleagues ask each other 'How are you?' each morning, but they don't really care. Their enquiry after your wellbeing is too often met with a polite but ultimately meaningless reply, as people aren't prepared to really reveal anything substantial or real about themselves. We also encounter insincerity when our customer service is delivered functionally, but lacks any warmth, empathy or commitment and customers sense a lack of authenticity in our actions. When this happens customers slowly begin to look for other providers who offer a similar product at a similar price, but with a service offered from an above the line culture that offers a genuine, warm, sincere and empathetic presence that makes all the difference.

Sense of rumour

A very strong indicator that a culture has slipped below the line, sometimes a long way below the line, is when humour disappears and is replaced by rumour. As a young anthropologist I was warned by my professor that if I ever found myself in a culture that lacked a sense of humour, I should take great care or get out. Cultures that lack a sense of humour have lost a sense of perspective and are liable to blow incidents out of all proportion as they cannot use humour as a safety valve. Rumour, on the other hand, emerges and becomes viral — very often with no grounding in truth or reality, just drama. Bad news travels fast and far, and rumours love to bring bad news. The real danger of rumours is that they favour drama over truth, so they lend themselves to exaggeration, untruths and deletion of facts, and as a result ensure people become misinformed and even disoriented. This can lead to increased stress levels, a breakdown in trust and communication, which in turn result in both a loss of job satisfaction for people and lowered productivity for the organisation.

Adopting a silo mentality

I'm sure you have heard of the idea of silo mentality. Nearly every organisation I have come across that has not committed to working on their culture suffers from silo mentality. It occurs regularly when a culture has dropped below the line. A silo refers to a department, team, function or project within a business that requires a particular focus or skill set dedicated to achieving a specific outcome. Silos are themselves useful in that they enable people to become extremely focused and productive using a specialised set of skills in an environment where they are surrounded by like-minded people and work together synergistically to achieve the desired results. The problem occurs when the silo adopts a mentality of separatism or elitism towards other teams, departments, projects or functions in the organisation. When a silo mentality is adopted, people experience a breakdown in relationships, communication and collaboration.

When things become extreme, I have even seen two silos become antagonistic and even aggressive towards one another. Some years ago I was asked to help a timber mill resolve silo mentality between two shifts that were responsible for ensuring the milling function in the organisation ran 24 hours a day and seven days a week. The two shift teams had adopted such a strong silo mentality between themselves that they both deliberately sabotaged each other's ability to work safely and productively. For example, one shift would hide tools so that the incoming shift would have to waste time searching for them before they could begin work. The creation of two teams was productive. One specialised in working at night with high tech-lighting and measurement tools; the other was adapted to daylight hours and used different equipment and lighting. So the silo focus of the teams was very effective and productive. It only became problematic when each silo adopted a destructive mentality or perspective towards the other team.

Attention turned in

Human attention tends to drift in one of two directions, known in corporate anthropology as In or Out. Attention directed in refers to the situation where people are thinking mostly about themselves. Their attention is locked in on sensing how they are feeling and what those feelings mean to them, why those feelings are occurring, and even how they feel about having those feelings. In below the line cultures people tend to direct most of their time and most of their attention internally.

Having attention turned in at times can be helpful and healthy, as it enables us to monitor our own energy levels or motivation and, if required, we can adjust these. Attention turned in can become an issue if it becomes a habitual way of viewing the world. In other words, most of the time a person or a team of people are solely focused on themselves. This quickly leads to acts of selfishness and a lack of empathy for others. Teamwork breaks down, and cooperation, collaboration and coordination issues become common across the business. In summary, some attention directed in is useful and healthy. But when it becomes habitual problems emerge.

Childish

Below the line cultures exhibit childish behaviours. Not childlike, as in simple and innocent, but childish as in immature. People sulk and pout, and withhold information, support and even friendship from one another. They engage in games: political games, manipulative games, and games of exclusion and deceit. It's incredible to watch mature, professional, articulate adults regress to being spoilt, sulky children who throw their toys out of their cots in fits of self-indulgent frenzy.

Reactive

When a culture becomes reactive to the world around it, and especially to a commercially competitive world, the culture and the business it belongs to are in trouble. It leaves the organisation vulnerable to change or competitive challenges—always on the back foot and unable to adapt quickly enough to meet customer needs or emerging trends in the market. A reactive culture is slow to react and tends to lag behind industry trends. It will also tend to be slow to respond to its own internal challenges or defaults.

Blame storms

People operating in below the line cultures are renowned for blaming others for their own shortcomings and mistakes. They lack accountability and ownership of their own performance. People will also blame circumstances and others outside their organisation for their poor performance. Anything that goes wrong will be the fault of competitors, the government, the market, the customers or the weather. In fact, they blame anyone and anything other than themselves. Management will be heard to blame their team members for lack of effort or application. Staff will blame management for a lack of attention and recognition. Everyone will be complaining about what they don't have, and I have often found that they exaggerate the impact this has on their ability to get things done.

Pessimistic

Given everything we have described so far about the characteristics of a below the line culture, it will come as no surprise to you that people tend to become pessimistic in these cultures. There's no hope, no point, no future and no help. Things will never work out well, and people won't believe things are achievable on time, within budget and to specification.

High staff turnover

Perhaps the most obvious and measurable aspect of cultures below the line is they have high staff turnovers. Even people who have recently joined the organisation will, within the first 21 days of starting their job, realise that, having experienced the organisation's culture firsthand, they have made a mistake. Even though they reach this insight within the first three weeks of joining the organisation, they will usually take up to two years to leave. During those two years they will be filled with regret, anguish, probably resentment and disappointment, maybe even stress. All of which bleeds into the toxic waste that has become the company culture, as the tides of doom and gloom sweep everyone away.

So these are the typical symptoms of a below the line culture, but what are the costs? How do all these factors influence the business?

10 costs associated with a below the line culture

Below the line cultures aren't simply something to avoid for your employees' sake. Below the line cultures cost your organisation in the following 10 ways:

1 Below the line cultures are by definition misaligned with your business strategy. The further the culture is below the line, the more misalignment to your strategy you can expect. Research has identified that, on average, culture has eight times more impact on your business results than the strategy itself. A below the line culture is pulling eight times more strongly away from your strategic objectives than the strategy is pulling towards achieving them. If you ever needed a business case to get serious and attentive to your company culture, this is it.

2 Below the line cultures have higher levels of absenteeism, which negatively affects productivity and performance. When people are away there is a double negative impact on productivity. First, there is the cost of hiring temporary staff to cover the absent. Second, the temporary staff are often slower to get the work done, as they don't know the procedures or systems as well as a full-time team member.

3 Productivity is reduced by a below the line culture as people withhold their discretionary effort. Discretionary effort is an inclination to give to the company and that decision is entirely based on the individual's goodwill, or level of commitment to the organisation. Discretionary effort, when given, is observed by others as someone going above and beyond the call of duty: people give their all and more. Discretionary effort is a sought-after contribution in organisations, as it regularly determines whether the goals and objectives, timelines and budgets can be achieved. Discretionary effort is withheld when people feel reluctant to give more to one another and the organisation or the customers when they feel they are at a disadvantage in the culture—when they find themselves in a below the line culture.

When the culture is experienced as taking from them, they are less likely to want to give back. As we saw earlier when reviewing the below the line culture traits, a sense of having things taken from you can occur in a variety of ways.

4 Below the line cultures have higher levels of staff turnover, which not only interrupts performance, but costs your business in advertising for replacement staff, recruiting, inducting and training replacements. Several of my clients have monitored and measured the cost to the business of staff turnover. In all cases my clients reported costs in terms of hundreds of thousands of dollars in small- to medium-sized enterprises, and millions of dollars in larger corporates and government departments. The resource website for human resource managers and industrial relations professionals, www.workplaceinfo.com.au, offers the following on indicative costs of staff turnover:

> A business with 500 employees can expect to have 50 resignations per year. Latest Average Weekly Earnings (AWE) figures issued by the Australian Bureau of Statistics (for November 2006) record AWE for full-time employees of $1058.90. Adding 30% to this for the cost of employee benefits and on-costs amounts to $317.80, giving a total cost of $1376.70. Assuming turnover cost to be a year's total remuneration for each employee, total annual cost of turnover for this business is $1376.70 × 52 weeks × 50 employees. That's a total of $3579420 per year. So a retention strategy that was able to reduce employee resignations from 10% to 5% per year would save this business almost $1.8 million per year, less the costs of implementing the strategy.

One of the most important and influential retention strategies is to develop a workplace culture that people enjoy and wish to belong and contribute to. A below the line culture sabotages such a strategy and reinforces people's desire to leave your organisation.

5 Below the line cultures have more communication breakdowns than above the line cultures, as they lack the necessary empathy to understand another person's or group's situation and viewpoint. Such breakdowns can cost organisations large quantities of both time and money. I recall an organisation

in the office supply industry I was asked to work with that had got to the point where different branches saw no point in sharing information with one another as they had all experienced the information being ignored, misunderstood or not acknowledged. The result was the loss of one of their major clients, as each branch was handling the client's needs differently, creating additional and unnecessary costs that were being passed on to the customer. The famous example of communication breakdown being costly was the NASA *Challenger* accident on 28 January 1986 that resulted in the death of all seven crew members. The resulting inquiry isolated an internal breakdown in communication as one of the most significant factors leading to the tragedy. In particular, it was revealed that engineers had developed a habit of talking *at* one another rather than *with* one another. The result was the emphasis in communication was on delivering data and information rather than understanding and clarifying how it had been received and interpreted.

6   Below the line cultures reduce customer delight. When employees don't want to be at work or do the work efficiently, effectively or gracefully, customers feel the difference and vote with their feet and purses next time they're in the market for your products and services.

7   Staff withholding ideas and suggestions is typical in a below the line culture. Just as people might withhold their discretionary effort, they might also withhold good ideas. If people feel the culture of the organisation is to take and not acknowledge or appreciate ideas, people will quickly withhold them. I came across an example of this recently while mentoring a senior leader who was fed up with the selfish nature of her fellow leaders. So much so she had all but made up her mind to resign. She told me that, during a leadership strategy meeting to explore ideas for cost-cutting across the business, she had withheld recommending that the company switch its courier provider to one her brother worked for, which could offer significantly cheaper rates, which would have resulted in annual savings of hundreds of thousands

of dollars. In particular she knew that two of her colleagues who reported to the board were likely to suggest the idea was their own, and so she chose not to share it with them.

8   Below the line cultures are renowned for theft, and the resultant financial losses: theft of materials, stationery, ideas, technology, furniture, morale and reputations. Along with higher than normal levels of staff turnover, theft is one of the strongest indicators that your culture has dropped below the line.

9   Brand erosion occurs in an organisation with a below the line culture. Brand equity is a process used in marketing to determine the value of a brand and is based on the idea that the owner of a well-known brand name can generate more money from products with that brand name than from products with a less well-known name, as consumers believe that a product with the well-known name is better than products with less well-known names. For example, the Apple brand was valued at $103.4 billion dollars in November 2012. Diversified conglomerate Tata group was recently declared India's most valuable brand, with a value of US$21.1 billion. When a culture drops below the line, it affects the value of the company brand, or brands. This occurs because a brand is not just a logo or a specific font and colour scheme: rather it is an emotional connection that the customer feels for your organisation or products. Company culture can and does play a significant role in defining that emotional connection. A brand creates a combination of expectations or promise in the customer's mind, and the culture can be thought of as the making or breaking of that promise. Branding is all about creating full alignment between your business processes and the corporate culture.

In the year 2000, when BP (British Petroleum) announced a major change in its brand promise from 'British Petroleum' to 'Beyond Petroleum', the result in brand value was significant. But the brand has become seriously damaged because of the major oil spill in the Gulf of Mexico. How did the spill occur? The culture was such that the organisation was not, as subsequent investigation has uncovered, fully committed or activated to deal with any potential catastrophic disaster. If it had been, then something as fundamental as a functioning shut-off valve would have become the culture's standard operating procedure. Beyond Petroleum was a brand promise to the market to be green, but it seems the business culture lagged far behind the promise. You might say that all business brands eventually morph to become the output of the company culture behind them. If that culture is below the line, brand equity will plummet. Brand is promise; culture is the delivery or sabotaging of that promise. If the culture is below the line, the promise is broken.

10   As we saw earlier while exploring the traits of a below the line culture, silo mentality can be very costly to a business. You will recall we learned how silos in and of themselves can be useful in an organisation, as they lead to focused groups of specialists doing what they do best. This increases efficiency and enhances speed of production and productivity. Silo mentality, however, becomes costly, as it leads to departments or teams competing with one another or contributes to a breakdown in communication, which affects productivity, collaboration and efficiencies, all of which can be extremely costly to your organisation as it takes longer to achieve results, and can require work to be repeated or at least double checked.

Having just finished reading through all the traits and costs of a below the line culture, you will no doubt need cheering up. You have two options. One, take a break from reading and go and make yourself a cup of tea and think of pleasant things. Or read on immediately to discover the wonderful, uplifting, reaffirming and powerful traits of an above the line culture.

Above the line culture traits

As you might expect, some above the line traits are simply the opposite of those that occur below the line. But some traits are not simply opposites, because an above the line culture is so significantly different from a below the line culture that mere opposites do not always occur. This is because, in an above the line culture, the perspective of work and life in general has evolved beyond that which exists below the line. It has matured into something more—something more liberating, powerful and hopeful, to such an extent that it is barely recognisable as something that is merely the opposite in nature to a below the line culture.

In many respects an above the line culture is unrecognisable compared with a below the line culture. To help understand how this is possible, let's explore the generic traits of a culture that is operating above the line. These are:

- giving
- fast
- sense of humour
- belonging
- attention turned out
- mature
- adaptive
- thought leading
- willing
- optimistic
- strong employee value proposition.

Giving

Giving is a simple yet powerful human trait. Giving is delightful for the giver and for the receiver. Giving is perhaps one of human beings' most precious characteristics in that it ennobles the individual from whom the act is delivered and humbles those on the receiving end. An above the line culture is full of giving, and gives in so many ways.

First, there is large giving—the giving that is the outcome of our collective endeavours in the work beyond just the products and services that are created as a result of everyone's efforts in the organisation. Products and services are the outcome, an outcome that even below the line cultures are capable of producing. So what we are referring to here is something more subtle than the actual product, and yet so closely aligned to the product or service that it is often seen by customers as inseparable from the product or service—so inseparable that its very essence is embodied within the service offering of the product itself.

I'm referring to the *intent* with which those products and services are made available or produced, and the manner in which they are delivered or provided to customers. You might like to think of the intent I am describing as the *attitude* that accompanies the creation and delivery of the products and services. That *attitude* is one of giving. In other words, even as the product is being designed or assembled or distributed by the organisation, the people carrying out these activities already have the end–user in mind. They can already appreciate and understand how the product or service will fill a need or solve a problem in the customer's world. They want to inject their work with the intent of service in everything they do with or to the product. In other words, they want to give their best as part of the creation and delivery of the product. The customer is often not aware of this background contribution as such, but they will appreciate or acknowledge the resulting quality of the experience they have with the product or service. It is this unnoticed application of skill and well wishes and dedication to detail or craft that transforms a simple product into a valued possession, a small work of art and a transforming experience.

If you have never worked in a culture that is positioned well above the line, you may find this definition of intent and attitude, of quality and craft, as a little vague and intangible. That's okay. As you progress through this book and begin to consider, observe and listen to your workplace culture, you will slowly find yourself catching glimpses of this subtle and ancient human trait. Interestingly, when I have tasked leaders to spend time looking for the evidence of giving occurring across their culture they often report back with emotional tales of unexpected generosity and caring they did not know existed in their organisation.

Another form of giving occurs in above the line cultures—one that occurs in thousands of small gestures and the language throughout every working day. This form of giving occurs when people give their support, friendship, encouragement, help, discretionary effort, ideas, suggestions, advice, feedback, recommendations, tips, guidance, patience, humour, warmth, even affection and love, to one another and the organisation's customers. This type of giving can be so numerous and common that it is easy to assume that this is just the way humans are when they find a culture worth contributing to. They can be almost taken for granted when they occur regularly. But they aren't—not really.

All you need do is ask customers who come into contact with such a culture and you will see their face light up with a bright smile, as they attempt to describe what they have experienced. They find it hard to do so, because while giving is a common occurrence in a culture positioned well above the line, customers spend a large part of their lives, their days and weeks interacting with other parts of society and with other cultures. So much so that when they do have contact with your culture they are delighted and at the same time a little lost for words. They find it difficult to describe what is so wonderful about experiencing your culture. They rely on lofty words to attempt to capture the essence of what they have touched. They will use words such as wonderful, delightful, surprising, incredible, rare, captivating and magical—wonderful words to have associated with your organisation and its culture. Words that are unlikely to have been the result of your business systems, processes and methodologies, but that occur as a result of your people being delighted to provide services and solutions to customers that they believe in. They see providing these services as an act of contribution to fellow human beings. This perspective will also be extended to their fellow workers and, if the leadership within the organisation has aligned to embodying an above the line culture, to managers and leaders. The culture is in such an optimised position that it feels good to participate in, contribute to and receive from.

All these varieties of giving occur in increasing levels of genuine generosity and regularity the higher the culture rises above the line.

Fast

The second attribute associated with an above the line culture is the speed at which it can function. Above the line cultures are free of many of the frictions that slow other cultures down. These frictions are described in detail in the next chapter, where we discuss below the line characteristics. This attribute of speed provides a powerful and significant contribution to productivity and performance, and ultimately enables a real competitive advantage. A culture with speed thinks fast, acts fast and manoeuvres quickly. Decisions take minutes, not days, weeks or months. Recognition of a job well done happens while the job is being done, and does not wait for a convenient time, or until the project is completed and measured on its final results. A fast culture offers aid and assistance to others before it is asked for.

A fast culture is proactive. It does not wait until a full-blown problem has been established within the organisation's world—a problem made all the worse by hesitancy and internal debate about whether any action should be taken and if so who will take responsibility and accountability if everything turns to custard. A fast culture races out to meet the challenge early, with commitment and confidence. With the knowledge it will not be judged or held to ransom for anything less that 100 per cent success, but rather celebrated for its quick thinking, for the courage to act and the willingness to lead the way in search of a workable solution.

In my experience a fast-moving culture is often able to meet the future at such a pace it can actually influence the future's impact on its chosen market. This can occur as anything from embracing new technology to providing customers with an improved offering or experience, to launching a thought leadership development program to support the organisation's subject matter experts to master the core skills to convert them from being useful to the business to being of value to the customers.

Fast cultures can seize an opportunity in the marketplace to provide a new or improved offering to customers, or to acquire another business to add to their growth, confident in the knowledge and, more importantly, the experience, that their own culture can and will move quickly enough to seize the moment and capitalise on it.

Slow-moving cultures are always vulnerable to changes in the marketplace or industry. They are also more vulnerable to broader changes in the world.

Sense of humour

I described earlier when discussing below the line traits how a lack of humour is common in below the line cultures. Cultures without a sense of humour have lost a sense of perspective and are liable to blow problems out of all proportion, as they cannot use humour as a safety valve. When humour is openly and frequently apparent in a culture, it is an important trait to take note of. The presence of humour in a culture is a sign that people are able to work with paradox. To understand a joke or even to find something amusing often requires people to hold two apparent opposites in place at the same time and use the contrary nature of the matter to grasp a new insight or perspective, and in doing so rise above an initial conflict. For example, if I share the rather lame joke, 'A horse walks into a bar and the barman says to the horse, "Why the long face?"', for anyone to find even some amusement in the joke they need to first deal with the paradox that horses don't go into bars. Horses don't understand sentences posed as questions, and a barman wouldn't talk to a horse in such a manner. The joke cannot only be grasped when these paradoxes are risen above and we concentrate on the pun. The horse has a long face both literally (a horse's face is long) and symbolically (suggesting the horse has a long face means it's feeling down, blue or sad and has come into the bar to drown its sorrows). My point? Humour in culture indicates flexibility of thinking, and the ability to lift one's own and others' spirits. My professor at university told my class of undergraduate anthropology students, 'Whenever humour is lacking for long periods of time, humans die. If not physically then emotionally and spiritually.' He went on to explain that when people do not have a sense of humour or don't laugh, they are often not really present to what is going on around them, even though they are physically present.

In organisations it has even been suggested by some business experts that not laughing is a symptom, or even a lagging indicator, of havoc in an organisation.

Several of my clients have demonstrated just how powerful a sense of humour can be. Kiwibank, for example, along with other banks in New Zealand, was asked by the New Zealand government to upgrade some of its systems to become compliant with new laws that would soon be introduced. Kiwibank had to cover more ground than many of their competitors as they were relatively new on the scene, having launched two hundred and eleven branches as recently as 2004. With a demonstration of what I can only describe as a remarkable example of an above the line culture at work, the people involved in completing the compliance project went above and beyond to get the job done. Why this extra effort? They didn't want to let their customers or the nation down as one of only two New Zealand–owned banks. The work, led by the irrepressible Richard Lorraway, the bank's chief risk officer, over a period of more than 18 months of concerted focus and application, was challenging and exhausting, and involved managing longer hours and frayed nerves. How did they manage this? They met the ridiculous expectation that the job could be done in time with a suitable and, as it turned out, inspirational, level of humour. Except on a few occasions when the going was particularly tough, the culture responded to the challenge by making light of the situation. As one manager told me: 'We knew we were going to make it because we could see and hear that people still had their sense of humour.' Perhaps we shouldn't be surprised to learn that the word 'humour' comes from the ancient Latin and refers to their humoural medicine, which taught that the balance of fluids in the human body, known as humours ('body fluids'), controls human health and emotion. We might interpret this as meaning that humour enables us to remain fluid and flexible enough to overcome or circumnavigate most of our toughest challenges.

Belonging

Where below the line cultures fracture into isolated cliques and develop a silo mentality, above the line cultures do the opposite and create a sense of belonging for everyone involved in the culture. Belonging in culture is central to culturing. The word itself sums it up perfectly: be-long. To belong in a culture is to have a sense of *being* in the right place, of *being* able to *be* yourself and to allow others to do the same. Belonging is a primal human urge and need. Our desire to socialise and fit in is hardwired into the brain, which captures the *long* aspect of the word. We want to belong for as *long* as we can. Be-longing is life affirming, psychologically re-affirming and emotively affirming. Above the line cultures offer this. The opposite is the isolation or fracturing of social groups into the smaller and often hostile cliques that are to be found in below the line cultures.

Attention turned out

As we discovered when exploring attention *in* as a concept, we discussed that human attention tends to drift in one of two directions, known in corporate anthropology as in or out. Attention directed in refers to the situation where people are thinking mostly about themselves. People's attention is locked in on sensing how they are feeling and what those feelings mean to them, and why those feelings are occurring, and even how they feel about having those feelings. Below the line cultures tend to experience people spending most of their time, and with most of their attention, directed internally.

With attention directed out the opposite is at play. In this case people are confident enough in themselves and with each other that they are free to allocate attention to the world around them. This one simple difference in a culture—between having attention in or attention out—has dramatic consequences for how the organisation operates. For example, with customer interaction employees who have their attention turned out have their full attention on the customer. Not half their attention, while the other half is already busy thinking of a response to the customer's complaint or enquiry. No: their full attention is given to the customer.

The difference is remarkable in terms of what the customer experiences. When I was working with Kennards Hire Pty Ltd, the superb Australasian family-owned business that provides hire equipment for thousands of people from every walk of life, I had the chance to present to all their branch managers at their annual conference. The essence of my talk was around the three elements that enable workplace culture to rise rapidly above the line (see chapters 14, 15 and 16 for a full discussion). One of the points I discussed was the difference between people having their attention in or out and the impact it can have not only for them as leaders with their staff, but also for their staff with customers. As part of my preparation for the conference I had visited a number of Kennard Hire sites to gauge staff behaviours and customer focus. The people were, in a word, superb.

As part of my follow-up process after the conference I visited a number of Kennards Hire sites a month after the conference and briefly interviewed customers as they were about to leave. All I did was ask them two questions: were they first time customers at Kennards, and how was their customer service experience. The responses were very telling. Those that were first time customers were understandably really impressed with the high standards of customer service anyone can expect when they visit Kennards. However, those who were repeat customers regularly mentioned that something had changed. They commented on how good Kennards Hire service had always been, but they believed it had somehow gone up a notch, which they hadn't believed possible. What had made the difference? What was it customers were perceiving and commenting on? Well, here are a few direct quotes from the customers themselves:

- Look, these guys have always been great but the last few visits, it's like they've tuned in even deeper to what I want and need. I can't really explain it but you feel really cared for.

- I'm not sure how to explain this. They've just got even better. I really felt listened to and appreciated. It's awesome. I mean, I'm not a big customer for them, but they still treat me like I am.

- Yeah, good, mate. These guys have always had their act together, but, yeah, I've noticed they just seem even more keen to help me out.

- English is not my first language, but when I come here it doesn't matter. They know my needs. I can feel they want to help me. It's very, very good isn't it?

Having your attention out is intangible stuff, but it gets noticed. It gets felt. People feel your care—they don't hear it or watch it: they feel it. Having your attention out is competitive and service gold. If you do nothing else different other than have your attention fully and directly placed on your customer during any interaction with them, and your competitors fail to do so, both you and the customer win. Customers comment on the feeling of receiving your full attention because it is a palpable experience that sits at the very heart of feeling served. Cultures that have attention out give a damn! And giving a damn gets noticed and commented on. It's not rocket science, but it is a useful and simple way to project your culture higher!

Mature

Just as children grow up through adolescence and on into adulthood, cultures can evolve to maturity. This occurs as social expectations require each individual to be and deliver their best in terms of being collaborative, friendly, committed, sharing, humble, effective and even forgiving of one another's mistakes or minor character flaws. A mature culture is a safe culture. People do not attack each other emotionally, verbally or physically. People act like the adults they are, rather than regressing into fear, anger and isolation. Mature cultures do not require the people themselves to be older; in fact I have regularly been in companies where the younger employees are more emotionally mature and handle themselves in a more adult manner than their senior or elder colleagues. Likewise I am not talking about people in organisations needing to be younger or more energetic and 'with it'. Maturity in cultural terms has nothing to do with age. It is about thinking with and acting upon many of the traits we are describing here as being above the line.

Adaptive

Above the line cultures are proactive. They do not rest on their laurels. They push their own boundaries before the marketplace asks or requires them to move.

Above the line cultures adapt more quickly than below the line cultures for a number of reasons. The most significant contributing factor that enables this adaptive meme to flourish is that in an above the line culture people's attention is not wrapped up and consumed by their own concerns. Their attention is turned out. To some extent, what enables a culture to be adaptive is that the culture has understood itself and is deliberate enough in all its actions and perceptions for it to be able to spend time on considering what is happening beyond its own cultural boundaries. This enables the culture to notice any changes or challenges that it needs to pay attention to and organise itself to consider and discuss or plan how to respond to these outside influences.

A topical and popular expression of being more demonstrably adaptive is that many organisations have turned to and embraced thought leadership to advance their own thinking and better respond to their customers' changing expectations and needs.

Thought leading

One of the increasingly popular and clear indicators of above the line cultures is the organisation's willingness to support the development of their staff to become thought leaders. When an organisation embraces thought leadership as a key part of the company culture, it is fundamentally declaring that it wishes to share its proprietary information and knowledge, often for free, to better serve the customer. If you're not familiar with the term 'thought leadership', let me quickly explain.

The term 'thought leadership' was coined by Joel Kurtzman, formerly editor-in-chief of the *Harvard Business Review*, in the *Strategy and Business Magazine* in 1995, to introduce an emerging trend he had identified of organisations deploying their internal subject matter experts to educate and inform the marketplace. Kurtzman further highlighted the rapid growth and application of thought leadership in his book *Thought Leaders: Insights on the Future of Business*, and commented how effective thought leaders were at introducing the latest thinking and ideas to guide customers to solve problems, or enhancing performance and productivity within the client's business. Since those early days, thought leadership has emerged as the 21st century's most effective process for building stronger, closer and longer-lasting relationships with existing clients and attracting new ones.

I have been fortunate enough to deliver an organisational thought leadership development program, based on the material from a book I co-authored called *Thought Leaders: How to Capture Package and Deliver Your Ideas for Greater Commercial Success* with fellow thought leaders Matt Church and Scott Stein. Organisations that choose to engage in this program do so for one reason more than any other. These organisations are fully committed to extending the manner in which they serve and add value for their customers. In doing so they also demonstrate they are not afraid of making their people the stars of their customer's experience. When I have run this program for organisations such as Canon Australia and Sugar Australia, they had no hesitation in selecting and developing their employees who had specific expertise, knowledge and skills and experience because they knew they would be of significant value to customers. In both organisations, they were willing to offer advice and suggestions that improved their customers' business and asked for no fee in return. Above the line cultures do this: they give in many ways with no expectation of return and ironically receive increased loyalty and appreciation from the customer. The end result is that the organisation endorses sharing, giving and adding value, and equips its most talented people to do so. All of which is in total alignment of an above the line culture: a culture that demonstrates it is totally committed to supporting its people to add greater value and delight the customer.

Willing

People who are willing are worth their weight in gold to organisations. To have a culture filled with such people and capable of attracting more of them is the dream of every organisation. Willingness has many expressions. A key one is that people make do with what they have got rather than wasting time, energy and morale complaining about what they do not have. Or blaming circumstances or other people for their challenges. Although not a direct opposite, where below the line cultures have blaming as a trait, above the line cultures have willingness. Willingness is demonstrated when someone does something that is not part of their day job, or position, but they see the need and jump right in to address a problem, or meet a challenge. Willingness is present when staff or leaders are asked to lend a helping hand or contribute ideas and, instead of moaning that the request is beyond their mandate or status or levels of enthusiasm, they apply themselves wholeheartedly to supporting the request. Why? Because that's what willing people do. And they do not do so in expectation of getting something back from you, or demanding that you help them later because they helped you earlier—they do it because they are themselves above the line. They love to contribute, to serve, to be involved and to be supportive. They believe in what the organisation stands for and the power of an above the line culture in which they feel like, and are treated as, active and important members.

Optimistic

Without doubt there is a clear distinction between above and below the line cultures when it comes to optimism. Above the line cultures are optimistic. It's not that being optimistic means people in the culture are delusional or have false and unrealistic expectations. Being optimistic in a culture means people believe that they will have the necessary willpower and collective esprit de corps to see themselves through. They take a glass half full view of life, even when the glass is three-quarters empty. Delusional—no. Dedicated and willing, almost no matter what the circumstance or challenge facing them—absolutely.

Strong employee value proposition

From the organisation's perspective, an above the line culture has the added advantage of providing a compelling employee value proposition. If you do not have a human resources department in your organisation, perhaps you are new to the term 'employee value proposition'. An employee value proposition is a series of reasons why anyone would want to work for your organisation above and beyond the pay they receive. This can include such offerings or opportunities as:

- promotion
- mentoring or training
- bonus incentives
- free health care or gym membership
- a fun, creative and productive workplace culture.

All such employee value propositions are enticing reasons for people to work for your organisation and stay with you.

A culture can quickly become well known in the marketplace as being one that is pleasant, exciting and rewarding to work in. The market reputation of a culture as one in which people are treated well by their managers and by team members quickly captures the employment market's attention and becomes a magnetic force. In organisations with above the line cultures I have seen a constant flow of curriculum vitaes arriving on the desk of the human resources director from people outside the organisation who want to be considered when a vacancy for their role or skill set becomes available. Let me be clear here. These CVs are not arriving because the company pays better than anyone else in the market or industry. They arrive because people hear or see how well people are treated by the organisation and, in particular, they want to work in an organisation with a positive and uplifting culture that is above the line.

All the other value propositions are quickly undermined and rendered of little value when the culture is bad. How is this possible? Because the benefits of an above the line culture are so strongly attractive to people. So much so I coined a phrase to capture the importance people place on the traits of a positive culture that I call 'cultural currency'. Cultural currency consists of all the benefits a culture offers to those who contribute and belong to the culture. Cultural currency includes such things as:

- warmth
- laughter

- friendship
- synergy
- encouragement
- listening
- sharing
- caring.

Hundreds of other experiences that people value could also be on this list.

Cultural currency does not belong to the organisation itself, but to the people who participate in and contribute to the culture. Cultural currency is like a second wage packet or salary, as it has such a significant role and value in their working lives. So much so that if the cultural currency is weak, as we would expect to find in a below the line culture, people find that their actual wage or salary is undermined and devalued by the fact they have to operate within a toxic culture in order to get paid. You might think of the situation as a formula:

$$\text{Wages} - \text{Cultural Currency} = \text{Value}$$

If the cultural currency is strong, then the value of the wage you earn feels as if it is worth even more because of the pleasant and uplifting environment in which it is earned. Cultural currency is such a powerful contribution to people's sense of job satisfaction that when it is weak, or lacking altogether, it is one of the most common reasons people give for resigning from their jobs. They don't describe it this way. You will never hear someone say the words, 'I quit. The cultural currency here is so low I'm losing value working here.' But you might hear them say, 'I don't like it here anymore', or 'The atmosphere (or energy) here isn't good.' I have heard people say, 'The culture here is toxic.' Unfortunately, because of the way in which many organisations go about developing their culture, they inadvertently communicate to their employees that the employees themselves do not own the culture—the organisation does. This is a missed opportunity, as employees then understandably expect the organisation (leaders, managers and the human resources department) to do something about the culture when there is a problem. When cultural currency is missing, employees in many organisations blame the company. As you will see later in this book, it is very important that the manner in which organisations approach the topic of culture makes it very clear to employees that they own the culture, not the organisation. A sense of ownership breeds a sense of responsibility and a willingness to contribute to make the culture better — to lift it above the line.

10 benefits of operating with an above the line culture

An above the line culture offers these benefits:

1 creates a largely social friction–free environment, leading to increased productivity

2 generates an extensive group synergy, enhancing collaboration, creativity and productivity

3 becomes a magnetic force attracting like-minded, talented people from the market, industry and beyond

4 retains staff for longer, saving money on recruiting and training

5 requires less micromanagement of staff by managers because of the positive and supportive environment

6 makes customer service a primary motivating experience for everyone, rather than a matter of compliance

7 aligns the considerable power and influence of the culture to the business strategy

8 enjoys free flowing and open communication: people feel safe to ask questions and clarify their understanding without the fear of being belittled in front of others

9 backs up and reinforces the company brand and the brand's promises to the marketplace

10 draws upon the huge amount of employees' discretionary effort in times of challenge or crisis, or draws upon people's talents and ideas to delight the customer through developing and sharing thought leadership.

Having explored in general terms the difference between a culture being above or below the line, let us review what we have learned by summarising the key traits in figure 4.1.

Figure 4.1: above the below the line summary

Above the line culture

Giving   Fast   Belonging   Mature   Adaptive

Sense of humour   Attention turned out   Thought leading   Willing

Optimistic   Strong employee value proposition

Misaligned to strategy   Fearful   Angry   Taking   Draining   Empty   Lost

Disingenuous   Sense of rumour   Adopts silo mentality   Attention turned in

Childish   Reactive   Blame storms   Pessimistic   High staff turnover

Below the line culture

Now we understand the above and below the line categories of culture, we can move on to investigate a variety of specific levels of cultures that occur in both.

We will start with three distinct types of culture that occur below the line: the dead culture, the dying culture and the disabled culture. In this way we will be lifting our inquiry from the lower to higher levels with each culture we explore. From there we will move on and turn our attention to three successful cultures. But first let's explore the below the line cultures.

CHAPTER 5

Below the line stages: dead cultures

The worst-performing cultures of those found below the line are what I call dead cultures. Now before I go on to explain what I mean by dead cultures, I want to be clear that this description has nothing to do with zombies. Stupidity, yes. Zombies, no.

A dead culture is one that does not exist anymore. It is a business culture that is already ripe for archaeological digs to go back in time and discover 'Who were these people?' or 'What went wrong here?' Dead cultures were once alive and kicking, but then got so toxic that the culture became like quicksand. A quicksand-like culture will quickly suck enough people down to the lowest levels of moral conduct and human behaviour. When this occurs the sheer intensity of these people's behaviours and choices begins to signal to others that it is okay to join them and behave as they are doing. Not everyone does of course. Many will quit their jobs as the cultural currency slowly destroys their soul. Others, the very bravest, will speak out or blow the whistle on the corruption or racism or sexism or bigotry that has emerged as a norm of the culture.

To understand what a dead culture is like we need look no further than the infamous case of Enron. I am sure you have heard of Enron, but if you haven't here is a short description of what happened. Enron employed nearly 20 000 staff worldwide and was one of the world's major electricity, natural gas, communications, and pulp and paper companies. With revenues of nearly $101 billion during 2000, Enron was named the US's most innovative company by *Fortune* magazine for six consecutive years. However, its success and fame went to the organisation's head. Gradually the leadership team became increasingly arrogant in their dealings with customers as they sought to meet their own bullish revenue targets. The acceptable standards of decision making and behaviours in the culture began to decline rapidly, resulting in increasing levels of corruption, including falsifying their financial reports with the assistance of their accountants at the Arthur Andersen accounting company.

What has the demise of Enron got to do with dead culture? Well, obviously the organisation doesn't exist anymore and so neither does the culture. But the more important reason here is that Enron was not put out of business by its competitors, and it was not put out of business because other organisations were undercutting their prices or stealing customers. Competitors were not delivering a higher level of customer service to the extent that Enron began losing clients. Enron was not providing inferior product in terms of the electricity or gas it provided. What brought Enron down was its culture! The fact that the organisation knowingly and institutionally behaved in the way it did over a long period of time shows us that the chosen behaviour and decision-making style and belief of the people within Enron, to think that it was acceptable to act in a illegal manner, set up a culture of dishonesty, complacency, superiority and arrogance. Not everyone bought into it: Sherron Watkins, the vice president of corporate development at Enron, blew the whistle on the whole affair. Until then, there was enough compliance and awareness within the culture to either look the other way or play along.

After the Enron scandal, boards of directors across the world began demanding that the chief executive officers and chief financial officers provide some indication of the nature and state of their organisation's culture, as they suddenly woke up to the fact that the company culture was powerful enough to bring their organisation down. I became very busy for a few years working specifically with clients who, after the Enron saga, wanted to get to grips with the nature of the culture they had generated in their organisations (often by default) and assess the impact of the culture on their business. In other words, culture had suddenly become to be seen by boards and then senior leadership teams as a risk factor, which many of them had never given much thought to at all prior to Enron's collapse!

The best thing we can learn from a dead culture is what *not* to do and who *not* to be. By becoming familiar with the traits of below the line cultures, we can begin to prepare ourselves to look for the signs that indicate that, if we do not turn things around quickly enough, the culture will die. Irish political philosopher and politician Edmund Burke once said, 'The only thing necessary for the triumph of evil is for good men to do nothing.' I would paraphrase his words in relation to culture and say 'The only thing necessary for a culture to die is for good people to do nothing.'

Organisations can be put out of business for all sorts of reasons. These could include a global financial crisis, better competition, fires, floods, wars or a shift in market trends and needs. Organisations' cultures only die when good people allow themselves or others to be anything less than their best selves.

Figure 5.1 (overleaf) shows us where the dead culture sits in the above and below the line cultures framework.

Figure 5.1: dead culture's position

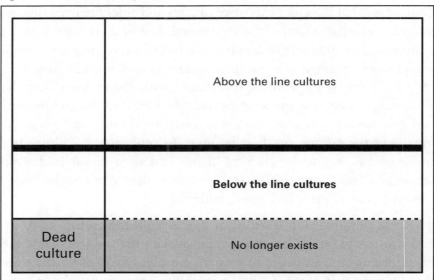

CHAPTER 6

Below the line stages: dying cultures

A dying company culture is a culture that is about to die and everyone can sense it, as the feel of the culture is bad — really bad. The sickness of the culture affects everyone and everything negatively, including customer satisfaction, employee fulfilment, management, productivity and leadership effectiveness. A dying culture can occur on a large scale, with attendant media attention and publicity. In more recent times than Enron, we have seen BP, Barclays bank, Citigroup, Goldman Sachs, JP Morgan and the Bank of England all accused of operating in a below the line manner. However, a dying culture can also occur in small- to medium-sized businesses. All that is required is for things to be bad in the culture and no-one being accountable or taking responsibility for doing anything about it.

The difference between a culture that is dying and one that is at the next level up in our review of below the line cultures is that, by the time the culture has reached the stage that it is dying, it is almost impossible to turn things around. This does not mean it is impossible, just very, very difficult and probably unlikely. Dying cultures can be thought of as the *Titanic* after it had hit the iceberg but before it sank under the icy surface of the North Atlantic Ocean — filled with dread, panic, selfishness, desperation and the occasional final act of heroism. In the organisational cultures that I have personally witnessed at the level of dying, some of the common behaviours I witnessed included:

- *Lies*. With the pressure on to achieve more when it is clear everything is declining (company revenues, productivity, performance, customer and employee satisfaction), people feel pressured to revert to lying or selling half-truths to protect themselves or buy themselves and their team more time. Leaders lie to the board about how well things are going, and then do the same to the staff, keeping people uninformed and only telling people, as one CEO told me recently, 'on a need-to-know basis'. The need-to-know basis he was referring to was to ensure no-one jumped ship prematurely before he could wring every last cent out of the business for shareholders before the ship went down. In true below the line style, he had also seen fit to organise his own life raft, in the shape of a similar role with a competing company.

- *Cheating*. This is about cheating the system, be it the tax system, the internal or external auditing system, cheating customers (for example through providing them with inferior stock or by fixing prices above their market value). It's as if, in a dying company culture, it suddenly becomes acceptable for people to be dishonest or sneaky, or even act illegally. Stealing company and colleagues' property may also occur.

- *Sabotage*. Of projects, company equipment and other people's property. Vengeance seems to be a big focus in a dying culture. Once people have awoken to the fact that the company ship is going down and they are going down with it, people look for someone to blame and then go out looking for revenge.

- *Ignoring others*. That can include colleagues, bosses and, worst of all, customers. People in this culture will ignore phone calls, requests for meetings and emails. They will ignore people standing right in front of them, trying to talk with them. When people exhibit this behaviour, it sends a message to everyone around them that 'I have switched off and I can't be bothered anymore'. And when we are ignoring, we are susceptible to becoming ignorant, because ignorant doesn't mean stupid, it means ignoring something or someone that could be helpful or useful.

- *Insults.* Insults tend to occur at this level of culture in all their various forms, and they will be directed at all sorts of people, inside and outside the organisation.

- *Backstabbing and blaming.* When things go bad a common trait in a dying culture is to make it somebody else's fault. The amount of both covert hostile behaviour and out-and-out hostility targeted directly at fellow culture members increases dramatically. This seems to occur particularly in cross-divisional or hierarchical levels of the organisation. The silo mentality we discussed earlier seems to kick into overdrive.

- *Cynicism.* This trait emerges and is directed towards the company leaders by the staff and at the staff by the company leaders. Both will often become cynical regarding the company vision, mission, values and strategic objectives as their own collective behaviour means they are falling far below the standards required to deliver on key performance indicators. They start to at first doubt the validity of the vision, mission, values and objectives and then move onto openly despising them and treating them as a joke.

- *Absenteeism and resignations.* Both of these increase: who wants to work in a culture like this?

- *Bullying.* A very sad fact of a culture that is dying is that bullying seems to raise its ugly head. It is as if the pressure and stress involved in trying to stop the organisational ship from going down is interpreted by some as permission to bully others. Just as blaming increases significantly across a dying culture, bullying seems to flourish in all its ugly forms.

Summary of culture traits at this level

All of the following culture traits may appear in dying cultures:

- ignoring each other and customers
- insults

- cynicism
- talking negatively about leaders
- very high staff turnover
- very high customer churn
- inter-departmental rivalry or warfare
- resentment
- lying to each other and customers
- very high levels of absenteeism
- disrespectful language and behaviour
- breakdown in friendships
- cheating
- blaming others
- negativity
- lack of attention to detail and the delivery of quality
- lack of attention towards other people, including customers.

The more of these traits that a culture manifests within itself, the more likely it is in its last days, and of course the presence of these traits actually accelerates the culture's demise. Things can be turned around, but this requires some drastic measures. We will look at how to achieve a culture turnaround in chapter 13, where I discuss cultural buoyancy devices. But for now simply learning to identify the symptoms of a culture that is dying is a useful level of awareness to develop and have on behalf of your own company culture. The trick to shifting your culture is to first see it as it is now. If you can see early enough that your culture is indeed dying, this offers the best hope of turning things around. The longer a company culture has to become habitually and unconsciously incompetent, the tougher it is to transition into an alternative and improved form of itself. Figure 6.1 shows us where the dead culture sits in the above and below the line culture framework.

Figure 6.1: dying culture's position

	Above the line cultures
	Below the line cultures
Dying culture	Decaying rapidly. Close to dying.
Dead culture	No longer exists

CHAPTER 7

Below the line stages: disabled cultures

Before we explore the traits of a disabled culture I will explain an important aspect of culture shifts that explains how a culture drops below the line to the level of being disabled. One of the reasons cultures drop below the line into the disabled state is because people do not realise that they are the gatekeepers of the culture. The moment people perceive that they are responsible and accountable for their own culture, it is very easy, you might say inevitable, for the culture to improve. Why is this? Because culture requires daily, deliberate effort and input to keep it alive and vibrant. The more deliberate the behaviours and language become within a culture, the more likely people will become conscious of the culture they have created and be in a position to point out problems to one another and adjust their approach as required. If, on the other hand, the culture is seen to be owned by the organisation and the culture is only considered periodically (let's say once a year through a culture or staff engagement survey), then adjusting the culture becomes too often a matter of too late and too little. It is harder to address a cultural pattern (known as a meme in anthropology) nine months after it has formed and become habitual. It is easier to pick up the early signs of meme development and bring it to your colleagues' attention to discuss and review the value of the shift, and the potential need for intervention. Because the culture has not yet descended into the dying status of our model, and if the culture is perceived by the people operating within it to be owned by themselves, then it is a relatively easy and quick process to turn things around.

For example, one of my clients, The Better Drinks Co, which creates and distributes the very popular drink ranges of Charlie's Orange and Phoenix soft drinks, were, under the inspirational leadership of the CEO Craig Cotton, going through a rebranding exercise. At the same time, they were moving offices and restructuring the business. Life at Better Drinks was busy. Craig called and asked me to support him and the team to focus even more deliberately on their culture. Craig and the senior leadership team had noticed that, because of the velocity at which the business was moving and the amount of change people were being asked to contribute to and handle, the culture needed attention to make sure it didn't drop a level. Because the team picked up the early warning signs typical of a disabled culture (listed at the end of this chapter), Better Drinks was able to quickly stabilise its culture and rise back to where it belonged—well above the line. The great thing about Craig and the team is that, even though they never fell below the line, they didn't wait for their busyness to drag them down but proactively met the challenge to their culture and won.

Owning the culture

The ability of a group of people to see and truly believe that they own their own culture often has to be initiated by the leadership team of the organisation. Because so many people have come to believe automatically that the organisation owns the culture, they must often first hear from the voice of the organisation—the leadership team—that this is *not* the case at all. When people hear from the organisation that the organisation does not see itself as the owner of the company culture, but instead sees the people as custodians and owners, the people who are so used to taking their instructions and guidance from the leaders will feel more comfortable and accepting of the new ownership perspective and opportunity to seize the day and seize the culture, and empower themselves to embody the culture and lift it up above the line.

The vast majority of employees are more than happy to discover that they own their own culture because, along with the customers, they are the biggest beneficiaries of a culture that functions above the line. The employees benefit first, and as a result of an increased sense of power, ownership and responsibility, they are then positioned to pass the benefits of the uplifted culture and all that that entails onto the company's customers.

The challenge in achieving this worthy outcome is for the leaders of the organisation to reach the natural and obvious conclusion that the employees own their own culture. Without this initial understanding and awareness by the leadership team, they are likely to continue to act and communicate in a manner that propagates the myth that the organisation owns the culture.

Understanding ownership for leaders

How do we ensure the leadership team understands this and communicates it across the organisation? All my experience has led me to believe that the only way to achieve this with a culture that is not already above the line is to hold a specific briefing or education session for leaders to make room in their spans of attention to consider this situation and understand the effects of continuing to propagate, even inadvertently, the myth that the culture is owned by and belongs to the organisation. The session should also be used to plan how best to communicate to staff that they own the culture, and when and through what medium this communication can occur.

A key criterion for a leadership team to be able to accept and work with this step is their ability to trust their own people. This may sound like a simple and even obvious statement, but it is not one that should be taken for granted. It can be a revealing exercise to conduct within the leadership team before even venturing into the discussion about culture, to ask your leaders to rate on a scale of one to seven how much they trust their people. Anything less than a high level of trust means that the senior leaders are unlikely to even trust their people to be informed that the people own the culture. This could mean the first step in beginning any work on culture is to work on and repair the trust that senior leaders have in their employees. If this is the case, the best place to start is to look in the mirror; leaders should ask themselves how they have allowed themselves to reach a point where they no longer have sufficient trust in the people who work with them.

Put the emphasis of the leaders back on themselves, rather than jumping into complaining about employee behaviour and attitudes. Leaders can ask themselves: 'How did the leaders of this organisation ever reach the state where the trust levels towards staff have broken down to this extent? How could this have occurred on their leadership watch?'

There is more to the ongoing process of moving a culture above the line than just looking at leadership and ensuring that staff are made aware that they own the culture, and we will explore the other steps in part III, but without this step all others are quickly undone, as the leadership are still seen as the holders of the strategic direction and political power in the organisation. Until the leadership are seen and heard to surrender the false premise of being responsible for the organisation's culture, any other action or plans to adjust the culture are only at the final discretion of the leadership team's approval and endorsement.

Having explained how cultures end up below the line in the first place, let's get back to our main intent for this chapter, which is to understand the traits of a disabled culture.

Disabled cultures

Without doubt, most organisational cultures that are in trouble—and below the line—sit at the level of disabled. This is actually good news, as with just a little more understanding and deliberate action and commitment many of these cultures could quickly lift themselves above the line. Disabled cultures have plenty to be hopeful about, as many of the characteristics that limit the culture are not difficult to fix and are often not as entrenched as those that occur when a culture is dying.

In the previous chapter I suggested that a dying culture has the impact of quicksand sucking people to lower levels of behaviour and moral standards. At the level of a disabled culture we might think of this culture as a road riddled with potholes. In other words some progress can be made, but it will be slow and uncomfortable, with many unexpected bumps along the way. It also can do considerable damage to the vehicle, which in this case is the organisation and its chosen strategy.

Disabled cultures have a variety of traits that are easy to identify — and people are more than capable of spotting these traits for themselves. Whenever I run an above the line session with organisations and teams, people can identify the disabled traits within the first 20 minutes of being invited to do so. Some of these traits will already show signs of being similar to those we listed at the dying level of our model. This is common. The process of dying begins early in a culture and if you know what to look for you can see the rot setting in even at the level of a disabled culture. In chapter 12, I will discuss in detail why behaviours and attitudes change as we shift between the various levels of culture. For now all we need to understand is that at the level of a disabled culture the attitudes and behaviours adopted by people reflect that the culture has dropped below the line.

Characteristics of disabled cultures

In the organisational cultures that I have observed at the level of disabled, some of the common characteristics included:

- *Arrogance.* We have all heard the phrase 'pride before the fall'. In using the word pride here I'm referring to arrogance and an air of superiority. I do not mean the pride people might take in their work or feel towards their organisation. Arrogance is a view of the world where the perspective of people in the culture is one in which they think of themselves as being better, or superior, smarter or more deserving than other teams, departments or branches of their own company. It may even mean they feel superior to their customers, so that customers feel belittled or looked down upon.

- *Rudeness*. In above the line cultures people are polite, friendly and civil to one another, but when a culture drops to the level of disabled people start to be rude to each other and sometimes rude to customers. Why is this? What triggers this sudden breakdown in manners? The answer is simple. Stress. It's like people driving in a quiet country lane on a leisurely Sunday afternoon, and doing so in a relaxed manner, but in the same vehicle they will often become stressed in busy traffic on a city freeway filled with drivers who are not really paying enough attention—and instantly the driver faces risk and danger. Road rage becomes part of their driving experience, both giving and receiving it. When a culture drops below the line to become disabled, the same thing happens. People feel threatened by the increased pace of others trying to make up for the drop in productivity and performance. People begin to feel stressed and short of time, which often leads to manners and etiquette being dispensed with in order to save time and energy. Unfortunately, this leads to resentment and adds petrol to the cultural fire.

- *Boredom*. When a culture drops below the line to the level of becoming disabled, people can lose a sense of pride in their work. They sense that the culture's and organisation's standards have dropped, and in response they become disappointed. Their energy levels begin to drop, which in turn affects others, who follow suit. For many people this unofficial lowering of standards deprives them of the desire to contribute as fully as they used to. They take a more casual approach. The buzz and energy of a group working synergistically to overcome challenges or achieve demanding goals is lost and boredom sets in, and people begin to smile and laugh less. The body language of people in the organisation signals, in a subtle and unconscious manner, that people are lethargic, uninterested and just going through the motions.

- *Customer complaints*. An almost certain feature of a disabled culture is that customer complaints increase dramatically, largely because customers end up bearing at least some of the fallout of people's stress and boredom. The service levels they were used to drop, due to the frenetic efforts of employees working faster than they should to deliver delightful customer service. Alternatively, the boredom of staff can be heard in their tone of voice, which is a turn-off for customers.

- *Higher absenteeism.* With the increased levels of stress in a disabled culture, employee absenteeism increases remarkably. I have come across levels of absenteeism in a disabled culture that are often three times higher than in a culture that is above the line. The cost to the business of absenteeism can be as high as those we considered earlier in the book relating to high staff turnover. In other words, hundreds of thousands of dollars.

- *Presenteeism.* Interestingly, accountants have coined the word 'presenteeism', which refers to the fact that although people are physically turning up for work they are not really applying themselves and often doing just enough to avoid getting into trouble or requiring any performance management. The accountants suggest that presenteeism can be just as costly to an organisation as absenteeism, as it also directly affects the company's levels of productivity. One of the early warning signs of presenteeism is increasing issues with punctuality at the beginning of the workday. When increasing numbers of people begin to arrive later and later to work, you have a plague of presenteeism at your doorstep. The best way to fix this is to get your culture back above the line.

- *Poor listening.* Probably as a result of all the traits we have discussed so far, and those to follow for that matter, people begin to tune out from both one another and customers in a disabled culture. The stress, boredom and presenteeism all contribute to lowered levels of listening becoming common in the culture.

- *Disengagement.* Although perhaps an obvious trait to associate with a disabled culture, disengagement is worth mentioning given that so many organisations conduct employee engagement surveys. If your results to these surveys are not favourable, or do not compare well with those in similar organisations to your own in your industry, pay attention. Your culture is probably at the best disabled—even dying, if the numbers are particularly poor.

- *Communication breakdown.* This is a hallmark of a disabled culture. Listening becomes an issue, but so too do empathy and sharing. People become less inclined to care about how others feel in response to the communication or message they have just delivered to one another. People fail to take into account what it must feel like to be on the receiving end of the messages they are delivering. This creates problems, as communication is really only as effective as it is received, and accepted or rejected. Refusal to share information or failure to translate your business jargon for the benefit of your audience's comprehension are both signs that communication is breaking down in your culture.

- *Squashed creativity.* Unfortunately, just when it is perhaps needed most, creativity and ideation are often squashed by pressing deadlines, stress levels, and breakdowns in levels of engagement and communication. In a disabled culture, birthing ideas is hard work and feels pointless. People feel they will not be heard or acknowledged so they simply don't bother.

- *Blaming others.* People sense that the company is struggling or collapsing and that the culture is fracturing with more self-oriented patterns of behaviour. Watching out for number one or your own team interests begins to take precedence over thinking about the wellbeing of the wider organisation. When people sense this shift, they react defensively and in doing so contribute to the problem.

- *Fear and negativity.* The biggest shift that occurs when a culture drops below the line is that fear emerges in the culture as a powerful motivational force. When people sense the organisation is in trouble, to varying degrees they begin to worry and panic. This fear drives people to behave in a more selfish manner and think and plan in shorter time frames. It also leads to people adopting a more pessimistic view of the world, the business, customers and each other. Fear is viral and spreads quickly, making nearly every activity that people engage in within the culture much harder to progress with than it need be. Figure 7.1 shows us where the disabled culture sits in the above and below the line culture framework.

Figure 7.1: disabled culture's position

	Above the line cultures
Disabled culture	Falling into disrepair
Dying culture	Decaying rapidly. Close to dying.
Dead culture	No longer exists **Below the line cultures**

CHAPTER 8

Crossing the line: a shift in perspective

The line is a turning point, a cross over and a transformation in a culture. At the line, people shift from being afraid and feeling hopeless, to become courageous and hopeful. They switch from feeling needy and taking from others in order to compensate themselves for what they perceive is missing in their life. Instead they embrace a new feeling of being empowered and resourceful in life. When people and a culture are rising and they reach the turning point of the line, they begin for the first time to consider giving instead of taking. They begin to see opportunities to help others, and give to others. People and cultures, once they reach the line, are ready to give as much as they take. Their efforts and contributions begin to be seen and acknowledged by others, rather than ignored and taken for granted. This feedback and recognition acts as a cultural reinforcement, allowing and compelling the people to feel better about themselves and perceive themselves in a more positive and contributive light. Even obstacles that, when confronted in a below the line culture, are met again at the line, they are suddenly no longer perceived as threatening and overwhelming, but rather as an invitation or opportunity for people to discover who they have become, where they are up to, and whether they can rise to meet this challenge. When a culture is at the line, a challenge is no longer seen as a negative or an obstacle but rather as a test—of people's unity, courage and resourcefulness.

So the crucial question we need to ask is why? Why is there such a dramatic shift of intent, awareness and behaviour when a culture gets to the line? The answer is a complex one that I will cover in more detail in chapter 13. But for now let me identify the underlying reason for this dramatic shift. At the line people's level of consciousness changes. I don't mean consciousness in any hippie, new age sense of the word. But rather as a physical expression of sensitivity and awareness of ourselves and our surrounding environment. This shift is dramatic and powerful. It results in people seeing the world differently, or, as we say in anthropology, 'adopting a new world view'. How does this shift in consciousness occur? As I said, more on this in chapter 13.

When enough people in the culture (in my experience as few as 30 per cent of the people in the organisation) feel that the opportunity on offer at the line is better than that they have experienced below the line, then, even though they are still experiencing work and the culture as challenging, they are not weakened by the prospect of having to face this challenge but are instead strengthened. They realise they do not have to face the challenge alone, and that the new sense of hope or optimism could be, and should be, enough to see them through if they only allow themselves to believe that tomorrow can be better than yesterday and that they themselves can be different.

The line and productivity

In straight business terms the line is a significant turning point for organisations, because it is only when a culture reaches the line that productivity occurs for the first time. As a culture rises further above the line, productivity increases often at astonishing rates, but prior to this point, all human endeavour in an organisation whose culture is below the line will be unproductive. Individual efforts that are productive may still occur, but these are quickly lost in the tide of unproductive actions and behaviours, decisions and intent, and vanish quickly below the waves of the ongoing wasted time and effort that dominates the culture.

How and why does productivity occur at the line? Because, as I mentioned, the shift in consciousness at the line transforms people's mindset and consequently the essence of their culture. People at this point feel empowered! This feeling of empowerment is a game changer, as it initiates a deep sense of both accountability and responsibility within the culture. For the first time, accountability is experienced as first and foremost accountability to oneself and then the culture that one is contributing to. Previously, accountability will have been to the boss, leadership team or the board of directors and shareholders. At the line, people become aware of their conscience and the possibility of doing harm to the organisation, colleagues or customers. They suddenly sense they have a sterner, more important test to pass than the need for revenge or selfish gratification: the test to rise above their own limitations and the collective fears of the culture.

Another important turning point that occurs at the line is the understanding of the connection between localised activity and intent within a culture, and the wider collateral impact the culture has on itself and outsiders. Another way of explaining this is to say that cultures below the line get caught up in the content of work and their work lives, and find it next to impossible to put this content into context. But once a culture rises high enough to be at the line, for the first time, people in the culture can begin to connect the dots and see how what they do relates to and affects people, both elsewhere in the organisation and externally (customers, shareholders, suppliers and society). They also begin to care about the consequences of this connection.

This has significant implications for leaders who are responsible for communicating the business strategy to staff as they will now have a chance of actually being attended to and even understood. In my workshop Communicating for Culture I ask leaders to become very familiar with this turning point of the culture as it enables leaders to have far more confidence that their messages are being received loud and clear and that they actually mean something to the recipients. In simple terms, the leaders learn that, at the line, their messages can begin to put the work or the business into context and they will be understood. When a culture is below the line, people, including the leaders themselves, tend to be predominantly still stuck in the content of work and fail to understand or really care about the overall context of how the work is contributing to a bigger strategic picture. This partially explains why silo mentality occurs below the line and not above. Silo mentality is the result of thinking and perception that is predominantly content based. It is only at the line that a culture can, as a result of a shift in perspective brought on by the increased expansion of consciousness, begin to grasp the concept of an overarching context for the business and the culture itself. Represented in a diagram, the communication process looks like figure 8.1.

Figure 8.1: the communication process

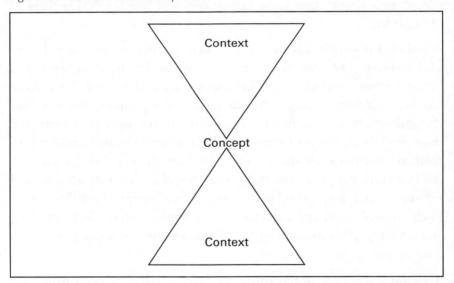

As figure 8.1 suggests, the content, in which the employees are buried every day in their work, narrows significantly as we rise up the triangle and draw closer to connecting with the concept of a broadening contextual triangle above. When the culture is below the line, the single point of connection at the apex of the triangle representing the content is still too low to touch or transcend the line. However, when the culture has risen to meet the line, the content triangle becomes free enough from its limitation of being content focused and exposed for the delivery of a new key message or concept to be received. This means the culture's world view has risen to a point where access to new ideas and perspectives becomes available. Suddenly a breakthrough moment can occur across the culture, because, for the first time, content can be connected to context and suddenly change becomes a possibility—cultural change, tactical change and behavioural change—a change in perspective. If you have ever listened to a great keynote speech or read a book or article that contained within it one message or point that instantly shifted what you knew about yourself or the world, you will know what I am talking about. In just a few short moments your view of the world changes, often never to return to its original perspective. When this happens in a culture, the transformation borders on being miraculous: a body of people suddenly have a breakthrough moment and not only see but also understand new possibilities for themselves and how they work and serve others. More than this, people actually begin, for the first time since beginning to emerge from the grip of the below the line culture, to care about seizing such an opportunity. Not just understand or acknowledge it, but care about it. In cultural terms, this is where the awakening of that wonderful human trait of empathy occurs. Empathy is critical in human relationships, as without it we would all be imprisoned in a perspective of the world of an entirely personalised nature. Community and culture do not begin to really function in a positive and empowering manner without the ability to empathise.

I want to emphasise the importance of this significant shift from being stuck culturally in a world focused on content to one that can perceive the surrounding context in which the work is being conducted, because some research has shown that only after thousands and thousands of years have some cultures been able to make this connection between content and context. Many still have not, and the same is true of organisations. Some organisations, for instance, continue to plunder the earth's resources with no thought for the collateral damage or future generations. The global fiasco that ended the subprime loan era that triggered the global financial crisis in 2008 is another wonderful example of the short-sightedness of an organisational cultural mindset so submerged in the details of the content that it remains blind to the wider contextual implications. You would have thought that the very words 'subprime' would have been enough to set off flashing financial warning lights, but when their heads are buried in a below the line culture, people are unable to lift their heads high enough to take in a fuller perspective.

So that is enough about being at the line. Let's grab our cultural passports and venture across the line for the first time and explore the empowering high performance world of above the line cultures.

CHAPTER 9

Above the line cultures: stable

We begin our investigation of above the line cultures with stable cultures. At this level, the culture is positive enough to be almost neutral in its ability or desire to do harm to the business, customers or itself. The people have liberated the culture from all the negative aspects of below the line cultures and at this point the culture seems almost to pause to catch its breath. A stable culture to a large extent just gets on with the business at hand without any great fuss or signs of resentment. There is no great celebration of the culture, or posturing through elaborate rituals or symbolic gestures. The culture just quietly gets on with delivering performance.

New behaviours

At least that's what it looks like on the surface level—the behavioural level of culture. Beneath, at the layers of values and beliefs, a quiet optimism has taken root in people's minds and hearts. However, they do not get carried away with this new sense of hope. It is almost as if they are not sure if the hope is truly present, and reliable and consistent enough to bank on its still being available the next day and the day after. But the very real sense of relief for people in a stable culture is sufficient for them to be empowered enough to begin to explore ways to contribute a little more in small, often unnoticed, ways to keep the culture afloat and above the line.

A key phenomenon that occurs for individuals in a stable culture, given they are free of the annoying, time-consuming and damaging traits of a culture below the line, is that they are drawn to the concept of integrity—integrity in terms of how the word is often understood to mean 'honesty'. They are also drawn to the more traditional meaning of the word, which is to be and feel 'integrated' as a human being. It is this self-honesty and desire to feel integrated and whole that enables the individual, and even the collective whole of all contributing to the culture, to contribute to the culture freeing itself from the characteristics associated with the pain and loss of a below the line culture.

It is at the level of a stable culture that humour is apparent. As we learned earlier, when humour is present in a culture, the culture is in good shape. As we discussed in chapter 4, the word 'humour' is from the Latin and refers to fluids and fluidity, originally in reference to the practice of medicine that paid attention to the condition and flow of fluids in the body. The reason the word 'humour' began to refer to what we now refer to as 'humorous' was that the ability to have a sense of humour (that is not to be funny, but rather to have the sensitivity to be aware that something is funny) was recognised as the ability to be fluid enough in one's perspective and thinking to circumnavigate away from or around a problem or challenge. Having a sense of humour meant that an individual could cope with paradox and rise above an apparent impasse to see another way to progress. In culture terms, this simply means humour and laughter are a real bonus as they enable the possibility of creative thinking and responses emerging within a culture.

The presence of humour is also related to another shift that occurs in stable cultures, whereby people's individual and collective courage emerges. It takes courage to lift up a culture from disabled to stable and, having tapped into the courage required to achieve this shift, people get to keep their newly discovered access to their courage and draw upon it whenever it is required. This is one of the main reasons why cultures that are above the line, when faced with the same challenge in the marketplace that confronts a culture below the line, always cope far better.

Courage is a universally celebrated and admired trait, so whenever the culture responds to challenges with courage it reinforces in a very tangible way that people are together in their time of need. Courage bonds people. Whenever we witness acts of courage in others, even if the action isn't real, as in a heroine in a movie doing something brave or a protagonist in a novel standing up to confront their nemesis, we as viewers and readers are moved—sometimes to the extent that our bodies physically react with goose bumps or by releasing tears of emotion. Acts of courage are driven from the heart, or what we believe in deeply, often at the risk of our own safety or our very lives. It is for this reason that courage is such a valued human trait in cultures all across the globe. To have people with courage present in your own culture is a gift. To know that you yourself possess courage is priceless, as it enables you and others around you to undertake tasks and challenges that people in below the line cultures could not bring themselves to do.

To help you put courage into perspective within your own organisation, consider some of the following questions. Ask your fellow workers for their opinions on the questions and I'm sure you will quickly begin to realise the power and advantage a culture filled with courage has.

- What acts of courage have you been responsible for, or have you witnessed, in your organisation?

- How do these acts contribute to your culture, business and brand?

- What happens when people lack courage in your culture?

- What are the consequences of lacking courage in your culture to your business and brand?

For some organisations, just reaching the level of a stable culture, if they have previously been below the line, is a real achievement in terms of the energy, dedication, personal sacrifices and willingness to not allow the past to be the governing factor in the future of the company culture. Many companies are more than happy to stop in terms of their progress with culture once they achieve the level of being stable. That is not to say they stop paying attention to culture altogether, but rather that they continue to do just enough to stay buoyant and above the line.

One final point that is worth introducing is that, having understood both the disabled and stable levels of culture, in my experience, the vast majority of organisational cultures fit at one of these two levels. At the risk of sounding a little melodramatic, I am on a personal mission to support as many organisations as are interested to shift their cultures above the line — and then perhaps onwards from there.

As I commented in my opening words of this book, I truly believe that organisations have a critical role to play on this planet of ours, particularly over the next one hundred years as we transition from the death and waste that seem to have contaminated so much of the last century. Organisations that have cultures above the line will be in a position to make wonderful contributions to the world. Those that still linger below the line will continue to act as a weighted stone around the mass of people who work for or are associated with such organisations.

At this point it might be helpful to recall that the means of supporting cultures to move from below the line to above the line, and in fact how to continue to lift the culture, will be discussed in forthcoming chapters. So having explored the first of the above the line cultures let's move on to investigate and understand the second culture in the progression above the line, which takes us into the realms of a successful culture.

Examples

Two examples of organisational cultures at the stable level include the following.

Kiwibank of New Zealand, given that they have achieved excellent growth since their launch in 2002. They have competed well with the larger banks in the market and coped well with the growth pains you would expect for a new bank, all while keeping their business culture above the line.

Canon Australia is blessed with world-class products, a dedicated leadership team and a customer-focused culture. Canon competes extremely effectively in what can only be described as an intensely competitive market. Many other organisations would fail to keep their culture above the line if asked to deliver the excellent levels of service Canon does, and compete as effectively as they do. The stress alone would cripple most organisations.

Summary of culture traits at the stable level

Let's conclude our exploration of a stable culture by considering some of the common traits we are likely to find present in such a culture:

- there is increasingly polite language and behaviour to colleagues and customers
- work ceases to be a drag
- there are initial signs of focus on work
- insults are no longer cast at each other
- smiling or laughing begin to occur
- people seem content in their work
- customer complaints begin to drop
- some signs of creativity begin to emerge
- some signs of collaboration appear
- lower stress levels and symptoms of anxiety occur
- sympathy for others occurs
- a sense of humour appears
- there is less hostility towards others
- courage appears
- employees start to become engaged
- there is respectful language and behaviour
- there is a willingness to communicate
- workers support each other and customers
- workers listen to each other
- there are increased levels of attention
- a cup half-full perspective appears
- people don't impede others' work
- there is quality in work
- a 'no one loses' philosophy emerges.

Figure 9.1 shows us where the stable culture sits in the above and below the line culture framework.

Figure 9.1: stable culture's position

	Above the line cultures
Stable culture	Absence of below the line traits
Disabled culture	Falling into disrepair
Dying culture	Decaying rapidly. Close to dying.
Dead culture	No longer exists Below the line cultures

CHAPTER 10

Above the line cultures: successful

And so we arrive at what, for most of my clients, is the objective of working on their culture: to lift themselves to the level of operating as, and perhaps even becoming known as, a successful culture.

The favourable reputation and status that often come with marketplace or industry recognition of a successful culture are not taken lightly by those who achieve such lofty heights. There is often not even a notable display of pride concerning the achievement. Rather there is a quiet satisfaction and ongoing commitment to do whatever is necessary to maintain what has been created to ensure that future generations of employees, customers, investors, suppliers, board members and shareholders all are able to draw upon and benefit from the culture.

Given that the culture has reached the level of being successful, you will also find that people within the culture have reached a point where they are constantly putting more into the culture than they take out. This has the remarkable and compounding impact of ensuring that the cultural currency becomes richer and broader in terms of what it can offer and how much it can offer to anyone associated with or participating in the culture. This willingness to give more than they receive is a hallmark of a successful culture and one that places this level of culture well beyond the grasp of many organisations. This does not mean that the level is unattainable—only that to achieve this level of culture requires a remarkable calibre of leadership, capable of the necessary humility and possessing the necessary skills and awareness to work with and communicate to the culture consistently enough and with the right quality to inspire the culture to respond. If this leadership presence is available within the organisation and married to the courage and willingness of employees to commit to and work diligently to the culture's higher possibilities, then not only is this level of culture possible, it is inevitable.

One of the reasons I encourage my clients to strive for this level of culture is that the rewards the organisation receives, and is then able to make available to all their key stakeholders, and especially customers, are well worth the effort. A successful culture is a culture filled with a people who possess a strong commitment and spirit of volunteerism. In a successful culture people have moved well beyond seeing particular jobs as being beneath them or their position. They will volunteer or 'muck in', as the common phrase goes, and lend a helping hand wherever and whenever it is required. This ability to foster consistent levels of volunteerism is particularly important for organisations based in Australia, New Zealand and the United States, as these nations consistently have some of the highest recorded rates of public volunteers in the world. What this means is that many people living and working in these nations regularly donate their time, energy, money and knowledge or expertise to worthy social activities. This includes everything from coaching junior league baseball, netball, rugby or soccer, through to volunteering as part-time community fire service or coast guard operations, helping out a local shelter or with the Salvation Army, or leading the local guide or scout troop. Of course, many people also volunteer in a variety of different ways to charities. The point being people in these nations will willingly give of themselves for something they believe in, so organisations operating in these nations really need to have a powerful and compelling mission or purpose for existing other than making a profit, if they want to really tap into the discretionary effort available to them from the local population. So, although organisations in these cultures have the luxury of being able to draw upon this willingness to serve, the trick is to not take it for granted or abuse it, but rather to align the organisation's mission to ignite this cultural tendency.

Mission and purpose

It is within a successful culture that a company mission statement or statement of purpose can become truly useful and influential in terms of inspiring employees and, perhaps most importantly, being authentic. There is nothing worse than announcing an organisation's mission or purpose only to find the culture is completely misaligned with these and the organisation quickly develops a reputation as being hypocritical—promising one thing but doing a thousand others. At the level of a successful culture, a mission or purpose statement can be easily aligned with the culture and the culture will deliver on the behaviours, beliefs and language necessary for an authentic delivery of the promises. You might even go so far as to say that only at the level of a successful culture does a mission or purpose statement really stand a chance of being taken seriously by the people in the culture. The reason is that, in a successful culture, the individual will willingly surrender many, if not all, of their egotistical needs to serve the greater contribution the culture provides to fellow workers, customers and shareholders. So much so that employees in a successful culture will often demand to have a mission or purpose, even if the organisation doesn't currently operate with one. This demand is driven by two factors:

- People want a unifying cause or objective around which everyone's unique and varied skills and abilities can be aligned, which offers a sense of cultural unity that departments or functions cannot.

- A mission or purpose statement actually provides a emotive connection between the culture and the strategy. This point alone often unleashes a huge amount of discretionary effort from the culture to drive the strategy far beyond where it was initially intended to deliver to.

In 30 years of observing organisational mission and purpose statements in all manner of organisations, I have yet to see one that is really taken seriously, or that activates and animates the people in the culture, unless that company culture was at least at the level of successful cultures. I would go as far as to say that, in a culture that is below the line, a mission statement usually becomes a mockery: values are violated, a strategy is sabotaged and a purpose becomes a platitude.

At the level of a stable culture, these things are not contradicted, but still to a large extent remain in word only. Elevate your culture to the level of successful and all such things spring into life. The talk gets walked, so to speak.

New questions

Unlike stable cultures, which tend to ask the question 'How can we fix this problem?', successful cultures ask 'What is the problem we are trying to solve?' In other words, they pose questions about the problem before they experience it. In this way successful cultures develop, in a small way, at least an increased capacity to meet the future and its challenges with greater agility.

Just as we have done for the other levels of culture, let's review the common cultural characteristics of a successful culture. Just to be clear: I don't mean that each of these cultures pose the questions of both 'How can we fix this problem?' and 'What is the problem we are trying to solve?' using these exact words. However, the nature of the questions and the intent of asking them are, in my experience, exactly as I have described. One addresses the immediate; the second, the immediate and the forthcoming.

Examples

Examples of organisational cultures at this level include the following.

Z Energy of New Zealand is a fuel distributor with branded service stations. Since Infratil and the New Zealand Superannuation Fund took over Shell New Zealand 2011, the new company, Z Energy, achieved its initial five-year objective in the two years of operation. The culture has played a significant role in the organisation's achievements.

Kennards Hire of Australia are well known throughout the country for their superb levels of service and commitment to the customer experience. Their motto, 'make your job easy', says it all, and the strong family culture can be experienced in any one of the organisation's numerous branches.

Bayleys Real Estate in New Zealand, committed to ensuring it attracts and develops the best real estate agents, places a huge emphasis on its culture. Led by the Bayley family, the company has an almost fanatical commitment to serving customers with passion, expertise and integrity. They constantly work on maintaining and developing their high-performing culture.

Summary of culture traits at the successful level

Let's conclude our exploration of a successful culture by considering some of the common traits we are likely to find present in such a culture:

- a strong sense of humour capable of seeing people through the toughest of times

- genuine friendliness towards others making the workplace feel homely

- clear communication including deep listening to each other and respectful language and behaviour. It also can include the verbal and written recognition and appreciation of other people

- engaged employees

- willing service

- attentive interaction with others

- positive perspective

- contributive approach to work

- success a common experience

- employees genuinely committed to serving customers and society

- bounce back from adversity in employees

- additional positive energy generated by the culture, which fuels individuals to contribute more to the culture, which lifts the culture even higher

- a win-win mutuality philosophy—treating others how you would like to be treated

- a significant shift from logical and rational thinking dominating the culture to a more balanced culture embracing creativity and intuitive suggestions to complement logic and rationale

- high levels of productivity

- blossoming of creativity

- work becoming deeply fulfilling

- work becoming craftsmanship

- genuine fondness for and friendship among colleagues

- smiling or laughing common

- people willing to face and address their own inner issues and flaws

- customers beginning to thank the employees

- collaboration sought and contributed

- minimal stress for employees

- people beginning to transition from being driven by external incentives to being drawn to be at their best by their internal values

- high individual self-esteem

- desire to compete replaced with desire to complete, on task and goals

- high confidence

- consideration of others becoming a natural way of operating

- giving with no expectation of receiving becoming common

- sympathy for others developing

- work beginning to be viewed as a personal development opportunity

- acknowledgement and respect for differing customer needs

- sustainability mindset emerging

- consistently high levels of performance.

Figure 10.1 shows us where the successful culture sits in the above and below the line culture framework.

Figure 10.1: successful culture's position

	Above the line cultures
Succeeding culture	The culture makes a significant contribution to performance
Stable culture	Absence of below the line traits
Disabled culture	Falling into disrepair
Dying culture	Decaying rapidly. Close to dying.
Dead culture	No longer exists Below the line cultures

CHAPTER 11

Above the line cultures: excelling

Before we even begin to explore the lofty heights of a culture at the level of excelling it is important to understand that, as compelling and impressive as this level of culture looks, it is certainly not for every organisation — for several reasons.

First, there may be no need to strive this high. The organisation and its customers and shareholders may find there is enough mutual benefit and advantage simply to settle at the level of succeeding. In fact, most organisations would benefit so much from achieving the level of a successful culture that there is no need to strive for anything higher, as the effort and mind shift required to do so may not, in the eyes of many senior leaders, provide a strong enough financial return. The second reason is that organisations may not possess the cultural capability to advance to the level of excelling. Bluntly, cultures that operate at this lofty height are filled with unusual people. I do not mean unusual in a derogatory manner. They are unusual simply because they are comparatively rare in the world of organisations. The degree of awareness, self-discipline and mastery that occur and are required at this level of culture are quite remarkable.

So be aware successful may be far enough for your organisation. Having said that, let's go ahead and look at the excelling level of culture.

New ways of thinking

I should immediately point out that organisations with cultures at this level do not think in the same way as cultures at any of the levels we have previously explored. A key distinguishing factor to recognise straight away is that excelling cultures understand the limitation of over-reliance on reason and logic as a useful means of understanding and connecting with people or the marketplace's real drivers. In this book I refer to this deeper insight as 'discerning the essence.' Essence is an awareness of what is really going on behind the scenes, or behind the comments or feedback of a person or conversation. For example, when a person in an excelling culture receives an insult from someone, rather than simply responding to or ignoring the comment, they immediately ask what it was they did or contributed to have offended the person and then either apologises or rectifies the situation or does both. Even people operating in a culture as highly developed as a successful culture are likely to meet the insult head on and consider the rationale or sense of the insult. An insult at the level of a stable or succeeding culture will be met with a question such as, 'Was that really necessary?' or an admonishment, 'Now that really wasn't necessary. I'm trying to help you here.' Or a challenge to the logic of resorting to insults: 'Look you can insult me all you want, but that's not going to help us resolve this issue for you, is it?' There is a degree of defensiveness or even of attack embedded within each of these responses. Whereas, at the level of excelling, the recipient of an insult is more likely to remain silent for a while, allowing the other party to vent their frustration, while internally they are doing one of three things or all of them:

- attempting to sense what the other person is feeling

- asking themselves what this person is really experiencing to prompt them to communicate in this manner

- empathising through association, such as thinking to themselves, 'Just like me this person becomes frustrated when they are not experiencing what they want and takes that frustration out on others.'

You may have found yourself in disbelief as you read through these three responses. You may even have felt sceptical or cynical. Perhaps you had some thoughts such as these:

- Come on you've got to be kidding me! Nobody has that degree of patience when they're being insulted.

- Right, so the people in an excelling culture are all saints are they?

- Sorry, but I'm not buying it. I have personally never come across such a culture. Are you kidding me?

- Yeah. See, I was rather enjoying this book up to this point, but now you have just gone from a useful business framework into la-la land, so I have to say I'm a bit disappointed.

I understand. They are uncommon reactions, aren't they? But that is exactly what makes these cultures excelling. They stand out from everyone else. They rise above the norm. They have taken culture where most organisations have never been or even dreamed it was possible to go. At the level of excelling as a culture, work is no longer really seen as work: it is seen as an act of service or as a passion, or the delivery of some deeply held sense of purpose.

A practical and wonderful example of this can be found in my own community. Just a few minutes from my home and office is a wonderful oasis of food, music and graceful service disguised as an Indian restaurant called simply Oh Calcutta. My wife and I dine at Oh Calcutta more regularly than I care to admit. After only my first visit I could see why the word 'Oh' was so applicable for the restaurant. Of course this was not their intent in naming the restaurant, but with every interaction with the wonderful people there, led by the beautiful and able Meena Anand and her graceful colleagues, the name is apt. On that first summer evening visit to the restaurant many years ago my wife and I found ourselves using that word 'Oh' repeatedly in reaction to the experience we encountered and became immersed in. Here are a few of those Oh moments that we still find ourselves expressing or hearing expressed when we visit the restaurant:

- 'Oh, how kind of them.'

- 'Oh, how lovely.'

- 'Oh, thank you so much.'

- 'Oh, wow, this is delicious. You must try this.'

This comment in particular gets used a lot at Oh Calcutta:

- 'Oh my god. This is exquisite.'

- 'Oh, how kind of you to notice.'

- 'Oh, perfect timing how did you know I was ready for another chai tea already?'

After dozens of visits to Oh Calcutta you begin to realise that you didn't just strike it lucky when you visited the first time and had such a wonderful experience. You realise that this level of elegant and yet casual experience is consistently available at the restaurant. I was intrigued about how they were able to achieve this constant level of customer delight and one day my wife and I arrived slightly too early, and the restaurant was not yet open. Being Oh Calcutta, we were invited to sit down regardless, and within a few minutes deliciously sweet and revitalising piping hot cups of tea sat before us. As I sipped on my tea I watched in quiet appreciation and fascination as Meena and Bhavana, her sister, gracefully worked their way around the restaurant lighting tiny candles at the feet of a variety of Indian deities that embellish the restaurant's walls. As each candle was lit Bhavana knelt with both hands clasped in a front as she whispered a quiet prayer.

I later asked about the ritual and in a very humble manner was informed that they were prayers of thanks for all the blessings bestowed upon all who owned, worked and ate in the restaurant. The positively delightful lead waitress, Bhawan, also explained that the philosophy played a central role in the intent behind the delivery of the delightful service we had consistently experienced. Bhawan explained further that the words '*Athithi Dev Nhav*' mean 'guest is god'. When I asked her to explain what this meant she explained that it meant that any customer could be an avatar (an incarnated presence of the Divine, here in human form on planet Earth). Therefore, serving a customer is elevated into a sacred interaction, as there is the possibility that at any given time as an employee in the restaurant you are serving tea to a divine incarnation. If you are from a Western culture this may seem a rather unusual if not extreme viewpoint and custom. If you are from an Asian culture it will be very familiar. As would the Hindu phrase '*Namaste*' used in greetings, which translates roughly into English as 'not for me, but for thee'. This is not a subservient greeting with a belittling of oneself before another, but simply a gesture of deep respect. Just as in some Buddhist cultures and parts of Japan, the bow is not a subservient gesture to another but a recognition of the sacredness of this moment, and acknowledgement that across all the spans of time this moment has never occurred before and will not occur again and that there is something either remarkable or even sacred about that. So the bow is not subservience to the other as much as it is subservience to the grandeur and scale of life and the possibilities of each moment.

The importance of intent

If you are wondering whether all cultures at the level of excelling must embrace some religious component, the answer is no. In fact, in my experience, few do. However, if you have ever experienced being on the receiving end of customer service that delights, not occasionally but consistently, where the people seem to have anticipated your next requirement almost before you have even realised the desire yourself, and each interaction with the staff seems to have a gracefulness or poetic delivery, then it can certainly border on feeling spiritual. It feels as if there is more going on than just the exchange of a product or service in return for your cash. If any of this sounds or feels familiar, you were probably interacting with a culture that operates at the level of excelling. There is something intangible and yet palpable about the feeling of such cultures, as if there is something in the air.

The source of this feeling, I have come to believe, sits squarely in the hearts of people's intent for doing what they do. It is not the doing itself—the hundreds of specific behaviours and gestures, actions and activities, instructions and dialogue you will experience in these cultures that defines them as excelling. Rather, the essence of these cultures is to be found in the intent behind each and every one of these actions, behaviours and conversations. This explains why describing cultures as the 'way we do things around here' is not really an effective way of defining a culture, as it places the emphasis of the nature of culture on the tangible, rather than expanding it to include both tangible and intangible.

One interesting trait I have noticed about excelling cultures is that they tend not to occur across or within very large organisations, simply because it is often a challenge to find people of this nature and consciousness in any large numbers. It is possible, however, to support and sponsor people in a successful culture to develop and surrender enough of their egos to float up in enough numbers to begin to excel. If you are patient enough and have permission to engage in conversations deeply enough, you will be surprised how many people would long to be part of a culture that excels. Perhaps this ability of even a small number of people to embody the essence of an excelling culture explains why anthropologist Margaret Mead famously offered small groups of people these profound words of encouragement: 'Never doubt that a small group of thoughtful, committed citizens can change the world. Indeed, it is the only thing that ever has.' Just because cultures at the level of excelling are often small by comparison with those at lower levels of our culture model does not mean they are any less capable. In fact Mead would suggest they are all the more so.

Another hallmark of excelling cultures is that, unlike any of the other cultures discussed, they will often deny that they are excelling, and instead profess that they have so much more to work on, so much more they could be offering. They do this, not out of false modesty or ignorance, but rather because they genuinely do wish they could offer more to others. In this respect they never rest on their laurels. Not that they themselves would say that, but they are always cultures that practice deep humility. This humility is a powerful contributing factor to what makes these cultures excel.

In other cultures there is nearly always some attraction or even necessity to prove someone or something wrong, which of course has the hidden and logical benefit of making the person or group that achieves this outcome right. In cultures at the level of excelling, right and wrong are seen as being less relevant than what will work. The conversations in an excelling culture can sound very similar to those that occur within other cultures, in that it can be perceived that the topic under discussion is just about establishing who or what is right or wrong. Listen more closely and deeply to the intent of every contribution, though, and you will quickly realise there is none of the usual to and fro or positioning to win that is practised in other cultures. Rather there is a unified effort by all those involved to find the answer that takes them forward as a group.

If you are unfamiliar with this sensation perhaps the insightful observation of my good friend and business storytelling teacher Andrew Melville may help. Andrew has made the distinction that there is a difference to be found in people's thinking and group dialogue that he refers to as Pole and Whole. Pole means the conversation or thinking behind the dialogue is stuck in a polarity, meaning it is rigidly binary by nature. This explains why the concentration goes back and forth as much as it does and often why at the end of the dialogue some have the distinct sensation they just lost something as a result of the interaction. Whole, on the other hand, refers to the fact that the group doesn't act think or feel as separate or opposed to another and so any idea suggested is tossed around and explored, not to discover if it right or wrong, but if it is fit for purpose. Does it fill the hole, just like a missing piece of the jigsaw that is being considered as the best gap filler?

Features of excelling cultures

In the last two chapters we discussed how a stable culture tends to ask questions centred on 'How can we fix this problem?', and that a successful culture asks questions centred on 'What is the problem we are trying to solve?' In excelling cultures the question that is posed is centred on the inquiry 'What is the question we are trying to answer?' Excelling cultures do not realise how different this line of inquiry is from those pursued in other cultures. In fact, I have often found they do not even realise they are approaching the inquiry in this manner. Yet the impact this type of question makes is quite remarkable. Let me explain. Before launching into your next business meeting think for a moment what would happen to that meeting if, after understanding the reason the meeting had been called, or you were all briefed on the meeting's agenda, as a group, you all simply paused for a moment and considered what question you were there to answer. If you came up with answers similar to the following, answers leadership teams have provided me over the years when I posed this question to them, then you will have grasped the benefits of this approach:

- creates real clarity on the why, what and how factors of the conversation

- saves large amounts of time

- builds an immediate sense of synergy among the group

- creates an ebb and flow of ideas that build on one another rather than contradict them

- dissolves any sense of hierarchy among the group in terms of addressing the question

- delivers better fit-for-purpose answers

- generates momentum, excitement, passion and commitment

- subtly regulates contributions in a neutral manner and tone

- is fast—much faster than most other approaches to meetings

- delivers an excellent rate of 'outcome achieved' ratings for meetings.

Finally, a real standout of a culture at the level of excelling is that they are extremely tolerant of people who are different from themselves. All the other cultures have a mindset that sees other people as being problematic in some way. Employees see customers as problematic; leaders see staff as problematic; and board members see the leaders as problematic. Not that they will confess to this perspective, but if you spend enough time in their midst and listen carefully and watch closely to reveal why they have designed their business systems, their codes of conduct, their governance protocol, their customer service approach, their human resources contracts and so forth, you will quickly discover that beneath all the activity, people are seen as problematic. This is what I was referring to at the start of the book when I said fundamentally I believe organisations do not like people. I still believe this to be true until you make contact with an excelling culture. So just as we have done for all the preceding cultures let's take a look at the common traits to be found in a excelling culture.

Examples

Examples of organisational cultures at this level include the following.

Oh Calcutta, Auckland New Zealand, for all the reasons discussed earlier in this chapter.

The one and only **Toms Shoes**. I can't do this company justice here, other than to say they sell shoes. Great shoes. And for every pair you buy they donate a pair free to someone in the world who doesn't have or cannot afford a pair. Check out their website at www.toms.com for a full appreciation of this remarkable organisation. No less than Bill Gates describes the company as the future model for capitalism.

The New Zealand **All Blacks** rugby team has the world's best winning record of any international and now professional sports team in any code, in all time. That didn't happen without having a fanatical commitment to culture. The culture in this organisation is legendary.

Zappos is the world's largest online shoe store and it is world famous in business for its remarkable fun and customer-centric culture. Amazon bought Zappos in July 2009 because it was reported they wanted Zappos for its culture.

Outward Bound, the New Zealand adventure school based in Anakiwa, uses the outdoors to challenge people to grow mentally and physically. The international motto for Outward Bound schools is based on some words from Tennyson's poem 'Ulysses': the motto reads reads 'To Serve, To Strive and Not To Yield'. This not only sums up the school's remarkably dedicated team, but also the spirit in which most participants at the school learn. Come to think of it, you could say the Outward Bound motto sums up all excelling cultures.

Summary of culture traits at the excelling level

Let's conclude our exploration of an excelling culture by considering some of the common traits we are likely to find present in such a culture:

- a real tolerance for people different from themselves. Gender, race, creed, religion. It doesn't matter which you are in most excelling cultures

- a commitment to equality. Human rights seem to sit at the very heart of these cultures

- employees who are purposefully engaged—these people are on a mission, which is always for the betterment of or in service to others

- empathetic language and behaviour—people in these cultures really care about their fellow human beings

- inspiring communication—the language in excelling cultures inspires the heart rather than just informing the head

- willing service based on a genuine enjoyment of people

- deep listening to other people's 'why'—like a succeeding culture, excelling cultures listen deeply to understand the other person's deeper motivation and meaning

- attentive and appreciative interaction with others, both customers and colleagues

- an optimistic perspective

- a creative approach to work

- a willingness and capacity to forgive others

- a shared sense of success

- judgementalism replaced by acceptance

- adversity seen as an invitation to express creativity and solidarity

- powerful positive energy, which is strong enough to deal with any challenge

- a win-win mutuality philosophy: treating others how you would like to be treated yourself

- creative thinking dominant over purely rational or logical thinking across the culture, enabling intuitive intelligence

- high levels of productivity

- an ability to see the whole picture that includes both the wider context and the detailed content of a situation

- work deeply purposeful, meaningful and motivating

- work as craftsmanship — people do not just do their job; they seek to excel in the role and deliver excellent results, products and services

- genuine fondness for and friendship among colleagues

- smiling or laughing common

- people able to face and address their own inner issues and flaws

- a 'wow' factor — customer service becomes customer delight when experienced through an excelling culture

- collaboration sought and contributed

- stress replaced by excitement

- people able to rise to personal levels of excellence through group symmetry

- collective self-worth

- competition seen as nonsensical

- clarity of perception is high

- consideration of others a natural way of perceiving

- giving is receiving

- sympathy for others has evolved into empathy with others

- a view of work as a privilege and the service of others as an honour

- an acknowledgement and respect for previous and forthcoming generations

- a holistic mindset

- consistently high levels of excellence and beauty embodied in the work

- an energised and yet peaceful and calming environment.

Figure 11.1 shows us where the excelling culture sits in the above and below the line culture framework.

Figure 11.1: excelling culture's position

Excelling culture	**Above the line cultures** The culture is the most dominant contributing factor to high performance and employee satisfaction
Succeeding culture	The culture makes a significant contribution to performance
Stable culture	Absence of below the line traits
Disabled culture	Falling into disrepair
Dying culture	Decaying rapidly. Close to dying.
Dead culture	No longer exists Below the line cultures

CHAPTER 12

A glimpse behind the curtain: consciousness and culture

Just take a moment and pause to reflect: are you enjoying this book? Have you learned anything new from it so far? Has it reinforced what you already knew and perhaps motivated you to continue with your efforts to inspire an above the line culture in your organisation, even though you are facing obstacles or naivety from your fellow leaders regarding your endeavours?

The reason I am posing these questions for you to consider is that in this chapter we are about to go deeply into the underlying essence of cultures. This is an important chapter to read and understand, but it may not be the best chapter to begin espousing or talking about with your more cynical or sceptical colleagues, especially if you have already determined, from your reading so far, that your organisation's culture is below the line. We are about to begin to consider culture as an expression of human consciousness. I know, I know—that sounds a bit woo-woo, la-la to most businesspeople. So before you hit the panic button, let me explain what I mean by the word 'consciousness'.

Culture and consciousness

When I use the word 'consciousness' I am referring to the human capacity to be aware. Imagine if for some reason you fell unconscious (a bump on the head, too much too drink, for instance). While you are unconscious you have little or no sense of yourself, your environment or others. As you regain consciousness, your perceptions begin to function again. Perhaps you can see, but things are fuzzy — you can hear, but noises seem muffled or as if they are occurring in the next room. Then, as your recovery progresses, your state of consciousness clears still further and eventually you have regained what you consider to be full sensory capacity. Only what you think of as full capacity is not your full capacity; it is simply your normal operating capacity. Your full capacity of consciousness is much, much higher than the one you normally function with.

Higher levels of consciousness give humans the opportunity to expand their sense of awareness in multidimensional ways. At higher levels of consciousness humans are capable of perceiving and understanding far more than they are at lower levels. This additional awareness changes who they are, because it influences their belief systems, behaviours, philosophy, language and thinking. It may not change the day-to-day tasks that people engage in, because, as the Buddhist saying goes, 'Before enlightenment, chopping wood and fetching water. After enlightenment, chopping wood and fetching water.' Meaning that the activity is the same, but the intent and experience of the activity is changed beyond recognition. How does this occur or is it even possible?

If we consider all human endeavour as an effort to influence our experiences, then how we initially perceive and approach, and even evaluate the outcome, all emanate from our level of consciousness. Consciousness is the space from which all our thoughts and actions arise.

If you consider this last statement for a moment, you can begin to see the importance of consciousness in terms of influencing the collective level at which a culture will settle. Individuals are attracted socially to others of a similar level of consciousness. When these social groups form, a culture emerges with its own sense of identity, mode of thinking and language. There is a scientific method to back this up.

Hawkins on consciousness

Dr David Hawkins dedicated much of his life to the exploration and understanding of human consciousness. As a psychiatrist, Hawkins approached the topic with rational and scientific rigour. He used the quite remarkable field of systematic kinesiology, which was developed by Brian Butler and based on the original creation of applied kinesiology by George Goodheart (1918–2008). Systematic kinesiology is a holistic therapy that uses the body's bio-feedback mechanism, through muscle testing, to gain information about a person. Hawkins and his research team conducted thousands of tests and after a period of time developed a map of consciousness, which operates on a logarithmic scale of 0 to 1000. Zero suggests there is no consciousness present; 1000 is gauged as the level of enlightenment.

In his book *Reality, Spirituality and Modern Man*, Hawkins says: 'there are actually two very different, diametrically opposed and polarized human cultures; those above and below conscious level 200'. Hawkins suggests that all consciousness below the level of 200 is collectively known as force. In other words, the levels of consciousness are grappling with, or are resisted by, restricted and challenged with force.

Hawkins describes consciousness levels above 200 as power. People who are at these levels are empowered and are able to experience themselves as being free from forces that dominate the lower levels of consciousness.

This clear distinction of above and below 200 levels of consciousness links to the levels of culture we have been exploring in this book. Hawkins suggests that it is naive to ignore consciousness as the dominant determining factor influencing human life and experiences. He contends that human consciousness is nothing less than the hidden determinant of human behaviour. Having travelled extensively around the world over the last 50 years and witnessed human beings at their collective best and worst, I couldn't agree with Hawkins more. Maybe it is no coincidence that we use the words, 'the *power* of love and the *forces* of evil'!

I have applied Hawkins's work and understanding in my own work as a corporate anthropologist for nearly 20 years now, and I have found his work to be the most effective way of supporting cultures to learn, shift and raise their levels of culture faster and with greater ease than with any other method.

A final, and important, point on Hawkins's research on human consciousness that ties closely to my statement at the start of this book that I believe organisations have a significant contributing role to play on the planet, especially over the next 100 years. Hawkins suggests that, for most of the time that humans have inhabited our planet, our collective consciousness levels have been below 200. For thousands of years they were well below calibrating, then as low as 90 at the time of Buddha, and climbing to 190 slowly over many centuries, until in the late 1980s consciousness finally tipped the scale and reached 207 for a few years, before dropping again to 204.

This shift to a level of consciousness above 200 couldn't have come at a better time. For the thousands of years that our consciousness levels were very low, life was short and brutal for millions of people. War, greed and man's inhumanities to man were the norm. Fortunately, during all this time we did not have the technological capacity to do deliver globally life-threatening weapons or products. Now of course we do.

Hawkins suggests that reaching the consciousness level of 200 was critical for our survival as a species, as without achieving it we would have possessed the means, the method and the motivation to destroy our world! Hawkins believes that only 15 per cent of the world's population has achieved a consciousness level above 200. That means that the collective negativity of the mass consciousness below 200 has only managed to avoid total destruction of many life forms because it is currently counterbalanced by just enough people above the level of 200 to make a difference. This is possible because the increase in power as consciousness rises is exponential. Only a very few people with high enough levels of consciousness are required to counterbalance the billions below. It is the level of consciousness that is the source of all human conflict, be this international or inter-departmental.

Raising consciousness

The good news is that consciousness can be raised. It just takes willpower and education on the importance of consciousness, mass consciousness and culture. This book has been written to make a small contribution to supporting organisations to raise their levels of culture and their levels of consciousness to better contribute to all and anyone associated with their organisation, as employees, leaders, providers, customers, shareholders or directors.

The intent of this book is to connect with anyone associated with an organisation who sees greater potential in their company culture, and both inspire and support you to begin to work with and educate others in the real power of an above the line culture to make a contributing difference. If you are up for this then the remainder of the book will show you how. If you are not, then please consider passing this book on to someone, anyone, who you believe would see the possibility in their culture and have the courage to begin.

Part III

ELEVATING CULTURE

EXCELLING

SUCCESSFUL

STABLE

DYING

DEAD

CHAPTER 13

Cultural buoyancy devices

Having spent some time exploring human consciousness, let's now explore the things you can begin to do to lift the level of your organisational culture. Over the following three chapters I will introduce you to the three cultural buoyancy devices. A cultural buoyancy device is a method for lifting the level of your organisation's culture. Each device offers a means of introducing, enhancing or accelerating the positive features of an above the line culture. You may not have to apply all three in your organisation, but I suggest that, if your culture needs to improve, then you will need at least one of them.

There are of course many ways of lifting the level of your culture, some of which you may have already initiated, and, if so, then more power to you. What I offer here are the three most effective means I have come across for lifting an organisation's culture. These cultural buoyancy devices are effective for a number of reasons, including the following:

- They make sense in the context of organisations.

- They are already at play within most organisations, but their level of efficiency and effectiveness can usually be improved.

- The organisation can take full responsibility and accountability for seeing them through.

- They are easy to apply.

- They are popular with employees and leaders.

- They make a noticeable contribution to customer delight.

- They improve productivity.
- They improve performance.
- They support the alignment of the company culture to the business strategy.
- They are great for the business brand.
- They can be fun to implement.
- They offer a distinctive and differentiating competitive advantage.
- They are not costly to initiate.
- Everything you require is in this book.
- Additional support is available online if required.
- The process is tried and tested.
- The process works fast—in some cases, very, very fast.

The three cultural buoyancy devices

The three cultural buoyancy devices are:

1 Ensure your leaders are worth following.

2 Make the work worth doing.

3 Create cultures worth contributing to.

Before we jump into the details of each of the devices, let me give you a quick overview of what each means and entails.

Leaders worth following

Leadership has a huge impact on a culture. When people in a culture perceive their leader as someone worth listening to and following, then the culture will align with the leader's recommendations, advice or instructions. So what makes a leader worth following? There are many things, but in my experience the most important are that the leader is credible and approachable, and they take culture seriously. We shall look at each of these in more detail in the next chapter, but let me provide you with a quick summary here.

'Credible' means the leader knows what they are doing. This can be as a result of previous experience, education or a combination of both. For example, I worked with Alloy Yachts of Auckland, who build some of the world's most expensive and prestigious super yachts. Many in the leadership team, although no longer physically involved in building the boats, had been boat builders earlier in their careers and so were well respected by the current carpenters and other craftsmen.

'Approachable' means being perceived as safe enough to approach for advice or direction, or even just a friendly chat. Mike Bennet and the senior leadership team at Z Energy in New Zealand became approachable leaders worth following when they undertook training to clarify their own personal values to enable them to better understand their underlying positive motivations to become even more people oriented. The leader's personal values have a huge role to play in terms of how they evaluate other people. Becoming increasingly approachable was extremely important to the leaders: they wanted to lead by example as they were about to invite the staff at every one of their petrol stations to put the 'service' back into their service stations. The staff at Z petrol stations accepted the opportunity and challenge, and are now recognised in New Zealand as consistently offering a warm, friendly culture.

Craig Cotton and the leaders of The Better Drinks Co did the same to clarify their own personal values in order to better understand what was driving each and every individual. Using the resulting insights, each leader was able to work on becoming better people and consequently leaders worth following.

Taking culture seriously

Leaders worth following take culture seriously and invest time and energy into the company culture to support the culture and optimise its own innate potential. Leaders that cling to the 20th century concept that culture is too 'soft, intangible, unmeasurable' to be taken seriously by senior businesspeople put their company performance at risk. The more leaders understand the role and power of an organisation's culture the more able they are to contribute to it, and in doing so earn the respect and willingness of other people within the culture to give their best. The Kennards family and their company's national leadership team have done this at Kennards Hire, by letting go of a perception of centralised control of the culture and by empowering all the branch managers and staff at their centres to take ownership and accountability of their local workplace culture. By encouraging the branches to take full ownership of the culture the family received unprecedented follow-ship from the branches, which committed and stepped up to make a culture that was already very good into one that was excellent. Alex Baumann at High Performance Sport NZ, ably supported by Susan Thomason and Chris Morrison, challenged themselves and their fellow leaders to become better at leading the culture and have done an impressive job of inspiring the amazing, talented and dedicated team to raise the cultural bar to impressive levels. Dave Rene and the incomparable coaching, playing and support group at the back-to-back champions Waikato Chiefs Super 15 Rugby told me that the role of culture sits at the very heart of the success story that is the Chiefs' recent history. By asking leaders within the squad to lead by example, the behavioural tenets that the team and coaching panel devised to bring out the best in themselves and the players have seen the growth of leaders worth following as they have aligned themselves around the leadership to deliver a champion team.

Work worth doing

It seems obvious to state that when people see the work they are required or asked to do as worth doing, they will apply themselves and their skills fully. It seems obvious, yet this concept is not as well understood as it could, or should, be in organisations. As you will read in chapter 15, this requires slightly more consideration and effort by the leadership team than simply producing a commercially disguised declaration of war though the company vision or mission statement.

Work worth doing has two key components that have to be embodied in the doing of the work. First, the work should be meaningful and contribute to something bigger than just the employees' contribution in return for a wage packet. Second, the work should enable or facilitate some experience of personal or professional growth for the individual.

Cultures worth contributing to

In chapter 16 we will explore what a culture worth contributing to consists of, and how contributing to such a culture can act as a cultural buoyancy device for the culture itself. A culture worth contributing to differs from a culture you belong to. Belonging within a culture offers a high degree of comfort: it feels natural to be in the midst of such a culture. Most people describe such a culture as feeling like home to them, or at least feeling at home within the culture.

A culture worth contributing to is different. In these cultures you the individual can see the greatness of the people around you and, rather than simply sitting back and passively absorbing everything the culture has to offer, you become proactive within the culture. You initiate conversations about life and experiences within the culture, in order to explore how things might be improved or simply maintained.

There are, of course, many things that make a culture worth contributing to and in chapter 16 I will highlight what I have found to be the most important and effective for creating buoyancy in the culture.

The three buoyancy devices that can lift your culture above the line are summarised in figure 13.1.

Figure 13.1: the three buoyancy devices

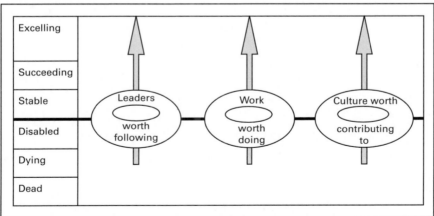

So let's get started with our first cultural buoyancy device, becoming a leader worth following.

CHAPTER 14

Leaders worth following

Are you a leader worth following? I ask this question in my leadership development programs. It's a confronting question, isn't it? Having leaders worth following in your organisation is critical for a culture to shift to above the line, or if the culture is already above the line, leaders worth following act like a buoyancy device to keep the culture afloat. To achieve this ability to act as a cultural buoyancy device, leaders require, as we briefly mentioned in the last chapter, three key elements:

- *Credibility.* The leader must be able to demonstrate that they know what they are doing, or are experienced in regards to leading a culture.

- *Approachability.* People must believe it is safe to approach the leader to ask for advice, make suggestions or ask questions about the approach being taken towards culturing.

- *Taking culture seriously.* The leader must demonstrate an interest in and commitment to ensuring a positive and productive workplace culture within the organisation.

The combination of the ideas and suggestions offered in this chapter will all contribute in some way to enhancing your ability as a leader in each of these three elements.

Are you a leader worth following?

So let's revisit the opening questions at the start of this chapter. Many leaders overestimate how worthy they are of following. They think they are doing a good job and are approachable, but when you talk to the people who report to them, you often get a completely different picture. This occurs because more than 75 per cent of leaders answer the question 'Are you a leader worth following?' based initially and primarily on their own perceptions of themselves. When I ask them to then consider the question purely from their followers' perspective, some do not know the answer or cannot adjust their perspective to answer the question, or they fall into the two polarities of 'yes, absolutely' or 'no, I don't think my team views me as worth following'. Again, the overwhelming majority give themselves a pass mark.

When I talk to the leader's staff members, the answer is usually the other way around. Not always, of course, but often enough for it to be worth investigating this topic further. I'm sure you can imagine that, when the majority of employees in a workplace culture do not perceive their leader as worth following, it becomes very difficult for the culture to operate consistently above the line. This is because a lot of the employees' energy gets directed into avoiding or counteracting the negative impact they perceive their boss is bringing into their performance environment. So instead of the culture homing in on its own power, it ends up fracturing in order to deal with the counterforces at work, reducing productivity, performance and fulfilment—all traits of a culture below the line.

So how bad is this leader-worth-following dynamic in the workplace? A survey conducted in 2012, commissioned by jobs website CareerOne, paints a worrying picture of leadership in Australian workplaces. The survey showed that 61 per cent of Australians polled say they have been bullied by their boss at work. Read that again: 61 per cent say they have been bullied by their boss at work! If that isn't below the line I don't know what is! Of course, whether they were actually bullied or they just perceived the interaction as bullying is difficult to determine and in fact doesn't matter. The very perception of bullying by a leader is enough for the people following to withdraw their follow-ship. The mere fact that a leader's behaviour could be perceived as bullying suggests there is something going on in the culture that will contribute to below the line culture traits emerging in the business. It could even be that there is actually no bullying taking place at all but people's self-esteem and comfort levels in the organisation are so threatened that even a genuine conversation with a leader in which the staff member is being offered guidance or disciplinary feedback becomes interpreted as bullying. But wait, there is more.

The CareerOne research reports that 37.5 per cent of employees reported being asked to do something unethical or dishonest. Twelve per cent claimed to have experienced sexual harassment. Overall, only 36 per cent of respondents rated their current boss as 'good'; 32 per cent rated the boss as 'average'; and a further 32 per cent described their boss as 'horrible'. It doesn't make for pleasant reading does it? When asked about their current manager, 68 per cent of respondents described them as people who kept them in the dark and held secrets. Again, we have to be cautious here, as many leaders will recognise what they can share with employees is sometimes legally if not commercially restricted. I have come across dozens of examples over the years where staff have failed to understand that their boss cannot reveal certain information to them, due to its commercial sensitivity and instead resent the leader for not sharing. A recent example occurred when a leader I was working with was asked by his team members if there was any news regarding the possible merger and acquisition the company was being considered for. The leader responded that unfortunately he was unable to share what he knew at that time, but that once he was briefed by the board and lawyers he would be able to share more. The staff immediately took offence that he wouldn't share information with them. The end result was that, legal and commercial sensitivity aside, the staff perceived that the boss didn't trust them.

In summary, the report suggested the top three horrible boss traits were:

- bullying
- belittling
- being moody or inconsistent, or both.

The top three qualities valued in a manager were:

- clear direction
- strong communication
- strong organisational skills.

Not all bosses suffer from the level of criticism and accusation suggested by the CareerOne research. In fact, when I first read the report I questioned its validity, given I had, in 30 years of doing this work, only occasionally come across situations where these behavioural traits had occurred. However, when I shared the findings with employee groups I work with to gauge their acceptance or dismissal of the report, more often than not they could relate to the figures. I was relieved to hear that, for many of them, these interactions had usually occurred at their previous place of work, which had provided the motivation for them to quit their jobs and apply for their current role. So it seems people are not afraid to quit a below the line culture to find an above the line culture to work in, as many of the people I interviewed or discussed this with in focus groups were doing the same or similar roles as they had in the below the line cultures.

So the question is, what can you do to ensure you are, or become, a leader worth following?

First, as I'm sure you are aware, there are hundreds of books already published on leadership, so if you are new to this topic, I recommend you explore this vast range of material. Online searches are a great place to start. You do not need to purchase anything initially, as simply reviewing people's recommendations for books on leadership and customer feedback comments can give you a better sense of what you are looking for or need.

In the rest of this chapter I offer some ideas that I believe position you as a leader worth following capable of contributing, to raising, or keeping your culture above the line.

Five ways to become a leader worth following

I have five suggestions that I have developed as a result of observing and supporting organisational cultural growth over many years. I have fine-tuned embodying and delivery these ideas through my cultural leadership development programs. The five suggestions are:

- pathway
- principles
- power
- presence
- perspective.

Pathway

A leader worth following must, by definition, be able to understand and clearly articulate (often repeatedly in a below the line culture), *why* the organisation exists, *what* it provides, and *how* it delivers or executes this. The number one criticism, without fail, that I hear staff members have regarding their leaders is their failure to communicate effectively why the organisation exists and functions, and what actual value it adds into the marketplace. So pathway simply means that a leader can explain in jargon-free terms to people across the organisation why the company does what it does, how the various resources, skills and people's efforts contribute to creating or delivering the company's services or products and what the service does to add real value to the customer.

Simon Sinek, in his book *Start with Why*, captures this concept brilliantly. Sinek uses the example of Apple computers and explains that their communication of their purpose is delivered in the following manner:

> Everything we do we believe in challenging the status quo, we believe in thinking differently. The way we challenge the status quo is by making our products beautifully designed, simple to use, and user friendly. We just happen to make great computers.

This is a perfect example of creating a pathway that both staff members and even customers can understand and buy into. It explains quickly in very simple and easy to understand words why Apple exists: because they believe in changing the status quo. How do they do this: by making beautifully designed, simple-to-use products. What are those products? Great computers. People don't buy what you do, people buy why you do it. When a leader can clearly articulate the why, how and what of the organisation, they become a leader worth following in the eyes of staff members, because so many leaders fail utterly to explain what we are all really trying to achieve through our collective efforts other than make a profit for shareholders. Explaining the company pathway can be a very a powerful and motivational narrative around which the culture can weave itself. Pathway narratives unite people's efforts and make the work feel meaningful. Leaders who know and share this narrative effectively stimulate a committed above the line culture.

Principles

The word 'principles' refers to what I call a time-tested truth. In other words, over a period of time an idea or a belief or a behaviour has been tested within the culture and found to work, and do so repeatedly. For example the principle might be to greet your colleagues first thing every day, as having been tested over time it has been noted that when everyone starts their day by greeting one another, the team works more synergistically and handles challenges with greater ease and grace. A principle delivers what we want and is reliable.

To become a leader worth following in an above the line culture requires a leader to be familiar with the key principles outlined in this book. The principles have, of course, been tested over time in many organisations and found to be valid, effective and true. The leader of an above the line culture would know which of the principles outlined in this book relate best to the context of their organisation and their desired culture. In understanding these principles, a leader places themselves in a position of being able to observe and communicate what works and what does not in regards to the culture. In doing so, the leader becomes of service to the team and the company culture by offering suggestions and ideas, or asking questions and listening to what can be done to fulfil people's requirements for job satisfaction, and also deliver the company strategy. In understanding the very nature of the culture that the staff members and leaders work within and being able to explain and communicate these to members of the culture enables the leader to become worthy of following due to their concern for the nature of the work environment and culture shared by all. In other words a leader who understands culture is understood by staff to care about them, their wellbeing and their job satisfaction, and this contributes to them being considered worthy of following. Key principles a leader might share and communicate to members of the culture could include:

- the link between strategy and culture
- the role culture plays in delivering on your strategy
- the concept of cultures existing only above or below the line
- the six cultures in the above the line model
- identifying where your current culture sits and where it needs to be
- the role of the three cultural buoyancy devices to support the lifting of the culture.

A leader, simply by demonstrating their awareness of the key principles of creating an above the line culture, becomes worth following because all but a few pessimistic staff members long to work in an above the line culture. A leader who is inspired by the idea of an above the line culture, who is willing to support everyone to achieve this outcome, is worth following.

Power

A leader must understand and appreciate the role human consciousness plays in determining the level of culture the organisation settles at. Human consciousness, when operating at levels associated with cultures above the line, is empowering! It enables more to be achieved by people with less stress and anxiety. It enables resolutions and agreements to be made more quickly than in cultures below the line.

Human consciousness below the line lacks power. Instead it relies on force to get things done or to be heard and acknowledged. Leaders worth following have to have a consciousness level that is aligned with an above the line culture. If the leader's consciousness level is below the line, it is difficult at best and, at worst, frustrating or impossible for the culture to rise above the line. Leaders in such a case are in effect endorsing a below the line culture. Below the line cultures never last long as they are destined to self-destruct. By understanding the role of consciousness (as discussed in chapter 12 in which I refer to the work of David Hawkins) a leader can communicate in the appropriate manner to maintain the culture's level or to inspire people to lift the culture higher. By becoming more familiar and effective with the understanding of consciousness as a real and propelling power, the better not only will your experience of the workplace culture be, but also your life in general. Leaders who understand this can champion and lead people to aspire to an above the line culture, which empowers everyone to experience better work conditions performance and job satisfaction while at the same time increasing customer delight. The higher a culture rises above the line, the greater both the number of people and the regularity with which they experience feeling happiness increases. Leaders who empower people to feel happy at work are popular and have little trouble being perceived as a leader worth following.

Presence

Have you ever felt, when you were having a conversation with someone, that they were really listening to you? That they were absolutely there for you, and in no rush to interrupt you to share their own thoughts? Did you know without question you had their undivided attention? If you have, you were experiencing what I call presence. Presence in a leader is when they make the other person feel as if they are the only thing that matters in the world right now. When a leader makes people feel this way, the people feel the leader is worth following. Let me be clear though. To attempt to pretend you care about people and pretend to listen to them in the attempt to be appreciated, liked and followed as a leader is a folly. People know when you're faking presence. The very act of pretending to be present with people in the hope that they will want to follow you is counterproductive. The process only works when you surrender the need to be liked or followed and instead just put all your attention on the people in the culture. Ironically, this in turn will deliver a desire to follow you. Striving to be present for personal gain backfires and delivers the opposite outcome. People sense your insincerity and resent it.

How then does a leader develop presence? The first thing to understand is that presence is largely an intangible quality. It is not so much a behaviour as it is a perspective. Behaviour plays a small role in delivering presence but presence is far more intangible than just body movements or just listening and asking questions. Presence is all about a leader's perspective, intent and attitude towards the people. The key perspective that a leader must have in order to embody presence is for them to perceive the people they are leading as great, or amazing or awesome. The leader must see the incredible power and opportunity the people represent. Sometimes they may have to perceive this before it actually exists! This ability or choice to perceive people as wonderful is important to becoming a leader worth following because it influences everything about how the leader interacts with the people for the better. The leaders are more attentive, the body language changes, for example, from being seen as from aloof or busy or disinterested to really caring. The tone of voice does the same. In seeing people as wonderful or amazing, a leader will begin to see the people not only as being worthy of their time and energy, but in fact that they are privileged to be leading these people. Feeling privileged to lead a group creates a sense of humility which in turn enables a leader to be more fully present with people and more willing to listen and really care about the other person and their feelings and ideas. People who perceive and experience their leader caring about them this much consider the leader one worth following.

Perspective

The old saying 'we don't see things as they are, we see them as we are', lies at the very heart of perspective. Perspective is a facet of being a leader worth following that is very closely related to presence. You may have even noticed that in describing presence in the previous section, I even used the word perspective at times to describe how a leader views or thinks of other people. Perspective refers to the viewpoint of the world and life in general and the people in the culture specifically. When the leader has a suitable above the line perspective of people, then they are likely to have presence. In other words in order to have presence a leader must first have an above the line perspective of life and the world. To develop such a perspective a leader needs to clarify where they view the world from. What are the specific personal values they operate from that colour the way they see life, the world and people? All leaders worth following have a very clear understanding of what they value most and how this influences their perspective of people. In understanding their values and their perspective, leaders are better equipped to self regulate and adapt their views to bring out the best in themselves when working with and leading others. A leader's personal values are the primary process through which they evaluate and judge others. When a leader knows their values and understands how they function and contribute to an above the line culture and motivate their behaviour and decision making, they are more likely to be able to manage themselves to act and operate with great integrity. Leaders with integrity are leaders worth following.

It's worth pointing out that these five traits may seem like a lot to work through, and in some respects they are. But I would encourage any leader who aspires to lead a culture that is above the line to pursue the embodiment of these five traits: I assure you every effort to do so will be worth it when you see the encouragement, empowerment and strength it gives people to create a culture above the line.

Having concluded our discussion of the first of the three cultural buoyancy devices, let's move on in our next chapter to explore the second cultural buoyancy device of creating work worth doing.

CHAPTER 15

Work worth doing

Every organisation I have ever been involved in, either as an employee or manager in my younger days, or as a mentor and adviser more recently, has recognised the importance of the work being perceived as worthwhile. However, not many have initially succeeded in creating this perception of their work. As with becoming a leader worth following, there are many things organisations can do to make the work worth doing. Many organisations, however, have to rely on some form of compensation to workers, simply because the work really isn't worth doing, or even if it is, the doing of the work is so demanding, belittling, exhausting or boring that the wage barely compensates for the sense of lost time and life doing the work. Wherever possible, and I realise it is not always possible, leaders need to try to create an intrinsic reason for the work rather than simply extrinsic compensation for it. Be aware also that the leaders' perspective of worthwhile work isn't always matched by the employees'.

Let me share a story. One of my clients is a Japanese-owned and -operated business with a global presence. The Japanese CEO in Australia was genuinely shocked when I suggested that the company's Australian employees may or may not be fully committed to achieving the results the business required for the coming financial year. His response was simply, 'But they are obliged to be committed!' I suggested that, in Japan, that was probably very common and, true, a sense of cultural honour alone would probably see to that. In Australia, however, the level of commitment was definitely going to depend on what effort and personal sacrifices were expected of people. In many workplace cultures, commitment can only be asked for. The giving of it is in the hands of those being asked to provide it!

How to create work worth doing

Here are some of the ideas I have found work best for my clients as means of supporting people to see their work as worth doing. They are:

- connect to something bigger—make the work meaningful in a way that goes beyond just making a profit

- aim for measurable progress—enable people to see how their daily work is demonstrably progressing their skill sets or experience

- learning and earning merit badges—remember Girl Guides or Boy Scouts, and the badges on the sleeve of the uniform; this idea can work in organisations too

- develop a prototype—job descriptions don't motivate people, but asking people to improve and update their job description does

- connect to personal values—work that does not align with our personal values is called a 'chore', but when work is a direct reflection of our deepest personal values, it ceases to feel like work and elevates to become a passion or a contribution.

Connect to something bigger

I count myself very fortunate and privileged to have as a client Z Energy in New Zealand, which took over the Shell Oil distribution business in New Zealand. Its wonderful CEO, Mike Bennet, is the epitome of a leader worth following. He is extremely well thought of by all the people who work with him. No one says they work for Mike, only with him.

He takes culture seriously and spends most of his time and energy serving others or learning how to be better at serving others. Mike is humble, smart and a deep listener. I have watched Mike with his people and when one of them is talking Mike gives them his full attention and soaks up every word. You get the sense that he's listening not only to what is being said, but *why* it is being said!

When Mike visited me for a day of discussion on all things cultural at Z, we talked about leadership, culture and strategy. Mike particularly enjoyed the discussion we had on the concept of commitment. As part of our discussion I said that I believed that for many people their job and work had become more than a money-earning activity. I believe many people see their work as a personal and professional development program. They are attending work to be part of something, to belong to a culture, to serve others, and to learn and grow. The fact that they get paid for all this is a wonderful bonus. Mike agreed and paused to think about the idea for a moment. He then said something I have quoted him on ever since. 'Yes, there's something in that. I mean on a bad day at work, nobody reaches into their office desk drawer to pull out their job description as a source of motivation and inspiration.' I burst out laughing, thoroughly enjoying Mike's insight. He was right of course. So what can leaders do to contribute to make the work worth doing?

Many attempts have been made to capture the worthiness of the collective efforts of everyone in an organisation in the form of a vision statement.

Vision versus purpose statements

Too often vision statements fall short of the intent necessary to lift a people to go above and beyond their normal day-to-day efforts and strive for and accomplish something quite remarkable. You can evaluate a vision statement for its likely ability to effectively lift a people and culture to a higher level of intent. Simply look at the statements and see if the intent is to serve others or contribute to making the world different or better in some way, or if it is oriented more to the organisation's own success. Any statement that has wording along the lines of the following examples will fall short or fail to lift a culture to its optimum level:

- to be the best in our industry
- to be number one in the marketplace

- to maximise shareholder return

- to increase our market share.

To support the development of an above the line culture, I recommend your company develop a mission or purpose statement instead of, or to complement, the vision.

A purpose or mission statement differs from a vision in one very important way. A vision describes a future outcome or objective you want to create or achieve, like those presented in the previous list. But some people may leave your company before the objective is achieved. For many people the fact that they may not be part of the culture when the goal is finally achieved can be demotivating. Why work toward something you won't get to personally experience? In workshops, I often ask people how many of them plan to leave the organisation they currently work for within the next three years, and more than 70 per cent of people say they do. So they often work knowing they will not be there for the long haul to achieve the company vision.

Vision statements

Many people simply find the vision of their organisation too boring or irrelevant to them to be motivating. For example, if the organisation's vision is to be the number one in their industry, many people look at the vision and ask 'Why?' Why do we want to be number one? They may wonder how that benefits them personally. Or what difference it makes whether the company is number one or number two. How will this market position change their day job? Does being a cashier in a supermarket ranked number two in the marketplace have a different daily working experience than a cashier doing the same job in the number one chain of supermarkets? Probably not.

Purpose or mission statements

Where a vision describes something that does not exist, a purpose or mission statement describes something that exists right now, that can be achieved today, and tomorrow and every day. This is possible because a purpose or mission statement outlines *why* we are doing the work today. For example, my client Emerald Grain, a premier grain merchant and pricing company in Australia, developed a purpose statement that said: 'Supporting Australian grain growers and their communities.' This purpose statement works because for every single person in the business this is what they do every single day, regardless of which role they work in. In this way, and unlike a vision which doesn't exist yet, a purpose or mission statement immediately aligns your culture to your desired stated intent. Emerald Grain doesn't have to grow bigger or more profitable to deliver on this purpose statement. People can turn up to work today and achieve the purpose together through the culture.

Another client, The Better Drinks Co, also has a purpose statement:

> Here at The Better Drinks Company—'Better' isn't just a word—but a promise and a challenge. A promise to give everyone a better choice, wherever and whenever they're thirsty and a challenge to deliver a better range and to be better at everything we do from sourcing and manufacturing to our final product delivery.

You may have noticed in both examples of a purpose statement the emphasis of the words is to serve others. This is important because to make work worth doing for people in your organisation, if the primary purpose of the work is service to others, your people will rally to the cause, because it will feel fulfilling and meaningful. As Aristotle wrote: 'Where your talents and the needs of the world cross, there you will find your purpose.' The best purpose or mission statements are simple and service oriented. Here are some more examples:

- IBM exists to foster the human capacity to innovate progress.

- Google exists to immediately satisfy every curiosity.

- MasterCard exists to make the world of commerce simpler and more flexible.

- We want Z to represent what New Zealanders can achieve when they put their minds to the things that matter.

- Kennards Hire exists to make your jobs easy.

- Emirates exists to connect people with the world through a new lens of perception.

- L'Occitane exists to share natural and cultural traditions.

- National Geographic exists to inspire people about the planet.

- Cultures At Work exists to inspire organisations' cultures to be above the line.

- We wanted to create a different kind of bank—one that provides Kiwis with a real bang for their buck, that has Kiwi values at heart, and that keeps Kiwi money where it belongs right here, in New Zealand.

- Apple exists to empower creative exploration and self expression.

- Outward Bound's philosophy and practice are designed to give participants greater insights into their own abilities and tenacity, summed up in Kurt Hahn's favourite expression 'Plus est en vous—There is more in you'.

- Qual IT: Our focus is to give you greater confidence that your IT project will deliver.

- Amazon exists to enable freedom of choice, exploration and discovery.

You might like to check out the lovely video on YouTube by Kiwibank which is so fitting for this chapter on making work worth doing: https://www.youtube.com/watch?v=Fm2uKTomUPk.

I realise that some readers may groan in cynical tones when they read through these statements, because they may perceive that such statements are too pie in the sky, or lack a hard-edged commercial proposition. Maybe they consider some of these organisations have drifted from their intent or that just because they have this statement doesn't mean that the organisations are what they claim to be.

Constant realignment

What I can tell you, as most of these organisations are or have been my clients, is that the organisations' leadership and employees are dedicated to constantly realigning themselves to achieving and delivering exactly what the statements claim, and most have done exactly that. They know that the statement alone doesn't do the job. It is simply their north star to which they realign themselves every day.

In his fascinating book *Grow: How Ideals Power Growth and Profit at the World's 50 Greatest Companies*, Jim Stengel provides ample evidence to demonstrate that development of and commitment to a compelling and service-orientated purpose actually makes good business sense. Stengel's research spanned 10 years and included 50 000 organisations. His research revealed that the 50 highest-performing businesses are the ones driven by a clearly defined purpose focused, in some way, on serving others. He also noted that these businesses on average grew three times faster than their competitors, and that investing in one of these organisations would have proven over the 10-year period of his research 400 per cent more profitable than an investment in the United States' S&P 500 stock market index.

Aim for measurable progress

In the 21st century many people see their work as a form of professional and personal development. That doesn't mean they do not take their job seriously or are not committed to delivering results. In fact you could argue the opposite. They are extremely committed to their work, as they believe it provides more than just a way of earning a living—they see it just as much as learning a living. For that reason it is very important that organisations, wherever possible, provide some form of measurable feedback for people in their roles as a means of enabling and encouraging people to explore and learn ways of improving themselves and their skill sets. The emphasis in this suggestion is on supporting people to grow themselves, and not just improve their performance and efficiency. The last two points are often the end result of such growth, but the people themselves are as interested, if not more interested, in the growing and learning process as they are the results this growth generates.

People love to track their progress. Some enjoy doing so by comparing their progress with others'. Some prefer to compare their performance with their own potential. Both work. The trick is to ask each individual which they prefer, as they provide differing motivational drivers. Making measurable progress is for most people deeply satisfying, and leads to a desire to learn and grow more, all of which contributes to making the work people are involved with feel even more like it is worth their best efforts. A simple and effective way of supporting people to measure their progress for themselves is to ask them to set goals and objectives related to their work. Alternatively, if they like to compare themselves with others, you might like to consider the process I refer to as merit badges.

Learning and earning merit badges

I am a big fan of the Boy Scouts and Girl Guides because their cultures are usually well above the line. They are adaptive. 'Be prepared' is a motto many organisations would do well to adopt in these volatile economic times. Both organisations also emphasise individual skill development, complemented by collaboration and team work. In my experience these young people often outperform their adult business counterparts in creating above the line cultures.

The process in action

I also admire the merit badge systems used by the Guides and Scouts. Asked by a business client how they could improve their ability to keep talented people interested in developing themselves when promotional opportunities in their business were limited, I suggested that merit badges might be a good idea as a means of supporting people to aspire to continue their personal and professional learning as they progressed through various projects. The client was Qual IT, which specialises in ensuring that organisations about to launch new software within their business or to the market have ensured it has no faults or viruses embedded in its coding. Qual IT are exceptionally good at what they do.

As part of an initial discussion with me, Steve Willsher, the business development manager, asked me which organisations I believed had the best culture that other organisations should consider copying or at least looking to for inspiration. I had already shared with the Qual IT executive team that benchmarking other cultures is in my opinion a flawed approach to developing an above the line culture. Without hesitation I responded 'The Boy Scouts or Girl Guides.' Steve thought I was joking and began to laugh, but then realised I wasn't joking and said, 'Okay, explain.' My key points were:

- Their motto 'Be prepared' is good advice for most organisations.

- They posses a real willingness to help and serve their community.

- They are committed and willing to build a strong positive and above the line culture.

- The culture makes regular and inspiring use of symbols and rituals to remind people what is expected of them as a guide or scout.

- Both organisations have a wonderful learning and development focus and use merit badges to celebrate achievement and motivate people to learn more.

I told Steve that I had been suggesting to a number of clients recently that introducing merit badges might not be a bad idea in organisations, given the desire by younger employees to stretch and grow themselves. Steve and his colleagues loved the idea and we talked some more about how, even though their business was growing, they still wanted to do more to keep the exceptionally intelligent team members with the company, given that promotional opportunities were not as readily available as everyone would have liked.

A few months after this discussion I visited Steve and the team, and they showed me a remarkable piece of work they had undertaken. Quite simply they had used their software expertise to create a range of merit badges that enabled employees to learn and study, with colleagues or senior programmers acting as mentors, a large range of topics—and in return they would earn merit badges that could be used to populate their résumés and track their progress in terms of leadership ability. The badges were available in a variety of streams, including core services, engineering, industry specialties and leadership capacity. I was stunned. The badges looked great and were comprehensively designed.

I told the team that this was capable of becoming a significant product range for them, as I was convinced that other organisations would fall over themselves to use a professional and skill development system that actually inspired employees to stay with the organisation and learn more! The Qual IT team wasn't overly convinced of the commercial viability to begin with. Every time I visited them I would ask how things were progressing, which, despite my degree of excitement for them, was slow. But they began mentioning to some of their clients, including the New Zealand Police Force, what they were up to and as you can imagine the interest was, as I had hoped and predicted, sky high. A short while later I received this email from Steve:

> I thought I should let you know that the Qual IT capability framework (AKA 'the badge system') has been going really well. When we last spoke we had launched it internally and our staff now use it to map out their careers and keep track of any evidence to support the badges they are 'earning'. We've just done a proof of concept badge system using a cloud-based application. We've been talking to clients about us hosting their own 'capability systems'. We've also mapped our badges to an industry standard for IT skills. At this stage we're just dealing with a Testing Capability badge framework, but we're mindful of the opportunity to extend this to other roles/skill sets and industries.

If, like me, you can see the amazing potential of this product, then you might like to contact Steve through the company's website at http://www.qualit.co.nz/contact-us/ to be kept informed of the progress on this product.

I can even imagine employees having real badges sewn onto their Qual IT shirts when they are based at a client's premises working on software quality assurance and the client asking what the badges are for. The answer of course could reveal another opportunity to serve the customer further. For example, imagine the Qual IT technician saying, 'Oh, that's my badge for integrating the new Microsoft software into your organisation's computer network.' And the client responding that they could do with help on that, as they hadn't been able to integrate the software as effectively as they would have liked.

In this way the merit badges become wonderful invitations to get into conversations about your organisation's expertise!

Closely related to this idea is my next suggestion for making work worth doing, which is what I call prototypes.

Develop a prototype

This is a simple idea and yet I have seen it add great value to employees' working experience, organisational productivity and customer service improvements. Here is the approach. As Mike Bennet noted, on a tough day at work nobody reaches into the bottom drawer of their desk to pull out and read their job description as a source of motivation. However, the job description can be useful if you ask people to develop a new prototype of an improved job description for their role. This simply involves asking people to audit themselves in their current role and while doing so make notes on observations and ideas for how the role could be improved or refined. Employees are the best people to ask what could be improved about their job and roles as of course they are the ones engaged in them every day. By asking them to develop a prototype job description, you invite people to explore and suggest ideas to advance, update or improve their job's efficiency and even their job fulfilment. Adjustments might include ideas such as:

- altering the hours of the role to better meet business or customer needs

- job sharing with other roles

- working remotely or from home for some parts of the day or week

- redesigning specific systems, processes and deliverables for improved productivity or outcomes

- briefing other dependent or interacting people or departments on how to better utilise the skills or services offered by the role

- redesigning or repositioning the physical location of desks, equipment or furniture for more productive outcomes, or to become more user friendly

- ideas and solutions to be delivered through extensions or adaptations of the role to enhance customer delight.

Once the job description prototype has been developed, it can be shared with the supervisor or direct report to explore the best ideas to implement and agree upon a plan or budget to carry out the proposed changes.

Connect to personal values

All the evidence shows that when people's personal values are aligned with their work the work becomes more consciously fulfilling. Inviting or providing the necessary time and support to encourage people to clarify their personal values always proves insightful and beneficial. People remind themselves of what motivates them and begin to see how the work they do or the organisation's purpose or vision statement actually means something to them in the context of their personal values. The more people are consciously aware of the benefits of their work to them and the positive relationship between work and the most important things in their lives, as determined by their highest-priority personal values, the greater levels of job fulfilment they experience. Personal values are a powerful source for both making work meaningful and for being motivated to work.

Personal values are also an important factor in the creation of a culture as they can be considered as the DNA of the culture. Personal values, when clarified and understood by people, inspire and equip them to see why and how they would be motivated to contribute to the culture. Personal values are the springboard from which we choose to belong and contribute to the workplace culture. In the next chapter we will explore what such a culture looks like.

CHAPTER 16

Cultures worth contributing to

To create a culture worth contributing to is easier and quicker than you might imagine. If people in the culture follow my five key stages outlined here you will go a long way in a short period of time towards initiating a culture worth contributing to. Let's look at each of the five stages in the order you should work with them:

1 ownership

2 decision making

3 commitment

4 communication

5 celebration.

I. Ownership

I have a saying I use a lot in reference to this first step of creating a culture worth contributing to: What we know is all we know. So I believe the first, and perhaps most important, step in initiating a culture worth contributing to is to bust some myths—to take what we know about culture and update it, rethink it and expand it.

Employees must know and understand that they own the culture. Most employees do not have this perception or understanding of culture. To help change this situation it is worthwhile for the leadership team to create and deliver a short TED-style talk (see step 4, communication) to bust the following myths:

- The organisation owns the culture.
- The leadership owns the culture.
- Human resources owns the culture.
- The external culture survey providers own and understand our culture.

Perhaps the most important point to make is to be clear that cultures are created by the people for the people. In this case that's you — the employees!

Reminding employees that they own the organisational culture is an obvious yet incredibly liberating and empowering insight for staff, as it makes them realise they are both accountable and responsible for the culture. Every time I have been invited into an organisation to make such a presentation the reaction from the gathered employees has been noticeable. Reactions have ranged from mild shock as people realise that they own the culture, to a sigh of relief or a murmur of excitement as they recognise they have just been informally given permission to get the culture to work functionally.

Sometimes it can be worth deliberately asking employees if they can see that the culture is theirs and that it belongs to them. Often this enables the group to open up and share some of their reservations about how things have been done regarding culture up until this point. In response, leaders can do as I do when asked to facilitate such discussions, and point out the truth in this feedback, which is why this session is being held, because anything that positions the ownership of the culture away from the people themselves is a fallacy and no doubt explains why the culture hasn't been functioning effectively in the first place. Now is the time and the opportunity to change that.

When people realise they have a decision to make, they can seize the opportunity to take their rightful ownership of the culture and begin exploring ways to shift it in a more positive direction, or they can continue with the status quo. In all the years I have been facilitating such discussions, I have yet to have an organisation's employees opt for the status quo of their culture. All have seized the opportunity to take responsibility and accountability for their culture. At this point we can invite their attention to shift to the most important and informed decision any group can make about their own culture.

2. Decision making

The decision to be made is whether employees want their culture to be one that operates above or below the line. To achieve this I suggest the leader of the people simply draw a line across a whiteboard and label the spaces above and below the line. They should then share with the people the fact that all cultures eventually oscillate and settle to be positioned as one or the other. Then ask them a question: 'What does your culture look like when it is above the line and when it is below the line?' Allowing for a few minutes', discussion, the leader can ask the group to share their thoughts and capture them on the whiteboard.

Once the board is populated with their feedback the leader should simply ask: 'Given you have now explored and owned the two options, which of these two cultures would you decide to create for yourselves?'

When employees decide whether they want a culture above or below the line, they have to commit to letting go of or surrendering everything they habitually or systematically do or think or feel that reinforces the undesired culture. They also have to commit to deliberately enacting anything that reinforces the desired culture.

A catch phrase you can introduce at this point to highlight the importance of surrendering the undesirable aspects that contribute to a below the line culture or elements of behaviour that are themselves below the line, even if the culture itself is largely above the line is this: 'You can be twice what you are by dropping half of what you're doing and being.' This means that the fastest and most effective way to double the ability of your culture to rise quickly to be above the line is to drop half of your attitudes, behaviours, habits and perspectives, identities and systems that keep the culture below the line.

A special observational note

If you watch a group of employees conduct this exercise — outlining their above and below the line characteristics — observe the behaviours and language they use to organise themselves and engage with the task and you will find yourself observing their culture at work right before your eyes. This can be very helpful in facilitating the group's understanding and learning from the exercise, as below the line cultures tend to overestimate their positive traits, and above the line cultures, through humility and a genuine commitment to improve, can underestimate themselves or be oblivious to their own above the line tendencies. This truth can then be gently shared to assist the group to get a bit of a reality check on their current situation.

When a culture is operating well above the line, the communication focus within the culture tends to be more conceptual and explorative. It is fast, creative and abstract. The conversations and communication flow quickly, freely and with great agility, as they do not need to be validated and challenged to the extent they would at lower levels of culture.

In a culture that is operating just below the line, you will tend to find communication, thinking, group organisation and language are slower and often more argumentative. These cultures often become more focused on exploring and describing the more mechanical, transactional and sequential aspects of performance and culture, rather than the values and intent within the culture.

This is because in lower stages of culturing, people tend to become trapped in the physical and material considerations of performance and culture. Whereas when the culture is above the line, these considerations have already been embodied and to a certain extent forgotten, although not neglected. This enables the freeing of communication to explore the metaphysical aspects of performance — the more intangible aspects influencing performance. In sport this is often referred to as being in the zone. In dance and music, it is referred to as being in the moment.

Pay close attention to language and communication and you will quickly see and hear the stages above or below the line that the culture is embracing through its use of language.

To conclude this second phase of the process the leader can ask the group I am facilitating for a show of hands to publicly indicate who is on board and decided to be part of the effort and inspiration for creating an above the line culture. The leader should encourage people to keep their hands in the air and then have a look around the room to get a sense of how much support there is for their endeavour within the culture.

Counterculture

Occasionally when taking people through the above and below the line clarification exercise described on the previous page, a small group of people may protest at being involved or even voice their scepticism at the possibility of anything changing. If this happens, try to be accommodating of their opinion and input because if most people are on board with the desire to move the culture higher it will probably happen. Even a minority of people can achieve this. I also recommend that you ask that the majority don't give the counterculture group a hard time, and suggest the group invite the counterculture proponents to join any time they sense or can see the group is making progress. Likewise, I encourage the counterculture group to be okay with their current opinion, as long as they do not deliberately sabotage the efforts of the majority, or become so stubborn that, despite the obvious progress being made, they refuse to join, and fail to benefit from the changes. Let's get back to the third stage in people working towards creating a culture worth contributing to.

3. Commitment

To be above the line and to stay there takes real commitment. There are five things a culture must commit to for it to even stand a chance of lifting itself, especially if it is currently below the line. The five things are:

- Commit to creating leaders worth following.
- Commit to making the work worth doing.
- Commit to creating a culture worth contributing to.

- Commit to creating a culturing plan (explained in chapter 17).

- Commit to inspiring one another to lift the culture above the line. How to achieve this is outlined at the close of this chapter.

4. Communication

Many leaders in organisations do not know how to communicate ideas explaining how to enhance a culture. They only know how to deliver information and directions, with occasional attempts at motivation (though most lack the skills, capability and willingness to convey these motivational messages effectively or regularly enough).

Communicating for culture is a specific approach to culture that involves both leaders and employees. For leaders it requires learning how to communicate for all audiences within the culture and to grasp that the symbolic nature of the message is more important than the rationale or point of the message.

To have a culture buy into, understand and execute messages or instructions from leadership, the message has to be carefully and deliberately constructed, and most importantly it must include an overarching metaphor. People don't remember messages well, but they do remember appropriate metaphors. For example, using the business phrase 'competitive advantage' may not linger in people's memory as the key point the boss was trying to make. But if the boss says, 'A competitive advantage is like being the fastest runner when you and a friend find yourself having to escape a hungry lion,' chances are the message will stick and as importantly can be retold again to others who may have missed the boss's initial message. Metaphors are particularly useful if you want people to implement your ideas or messages once they are back at their work station or department.

Communicating for culture is a skill set and technique worth learning and mastering if you want to play your part in elevating the culture as part of being a leader worth following. Some of this learning is simple. For example, emulating the design and delivery of a TED-style talk. TED talks are no more than 18 minutes, and they are delivered with passion, clarity and a strong and empowering message, often accompanied by simple graphic images. Not death by PowerPoint. TED talks work well because they are entertaining, informative and aimed at delivering a single message. These meet all the necessary criteria of a modern business audience that are distracted, possibly disinterested, and just too busy to take on too much information and remember it.

TED stands for Technology, Entertainment, Design and is an annual conference held in California in which some of the world's most innovative and creative people share their ideas, stories, philosophies and research in an entertaining, insightful and motivating manner. Check out TED.com. If you do not know about TED you are in for a treat. I warn you that if you do visit the site remember to inform your family they may not see you for a few days, as the website and the talks are highly addictive, in the nicest possible way.

One of the simplest and most effective techniques is a process developed by organisational culture expert Professor Edgar Schein, who identified the three aspects of culture that distinguished the visible from the underlying invisible and motivational part of culture. The technique is called 'humble inquiry: the gentle art of asking instead of telling'. It highlights the point that communication is essential in a healthy organisation. But often when we interact with other people, especially those who report to us, we simply tell them what we think they need to know. The result of this, from a cultural point of view, is that we shut them down and undermine their opportunity to contribute their creativity and new ideas, and to develop agility and flexibility in their own thinking and practices.

Schein defines humble inquiry as:

> the fine art of drawing someone out, of asking questions to which you do not know the answer, of building a relationship based on curiosity and interest in the other person.

Humble inquiry contrasts with other kinds of inquiry in that it builds rather than undermines a culture. It also works well in many different settings, and enables leaders to overcome the cultural and organisational barriers that keep us from delivering a culture above the line. Although not rocket science — it simply requires asking as the preferred method of communicating over telling — and the fact it is very easy to learn and quick to apply, it is so counterintuitive for many leaders that my communication workshop enables them to transfer the theory, and although they grasp the concept quickly, they often need some practice for it to become a natural way of communicating.

In regards to employees communicating to support the culture, the following guidelines are suggested:

- Be polite.

- Be positive in your communication.

- Talk it up. 'It' being the culture.

- Remind each other of the commitment made to create and deliver a culture above the line.

- Thank each another for your efforts, contribution, kind words, involvement or friendship.

5. Celebration

Celebration within a culture plays a significant role in reinforcing the culture and reminding people why they have chosen to contribute fully. There are a variety of ways a culture can celebrate itself, which include:

- using relevant symbols, such as the company logo, or mission or purpose statements or statements of company values

- holding company conferences that don't simply celebrate results and performance but rather the culture 'we have created together'

- celebrating heroes within the culture who have demonstrated and embodied the deepest values of the culture, even in the face of overwhelming circumstances or odds

- developing and practising relevant rituals as a powerful way of celebrating a culture.

Celebrating the success of your culture is really important, as it reminds people of just how much can be achieved when they all work together. I recommend that you celebrate the workplace culture once or twice a year with some type of semi-formal or formal event. It needn't be expensive or time consuming. It just requires a pause in the work activity or at the beginning or end of a work day to reflect and share on what makes the culture worth belonging and contributing to. A great way to achieve this is for people to be invited to share their favourite story about the culture. Perhaps they can describe how the team's sense of humour got them through a tough challenge. Or maybe how the team rallied around each other and supported one another and the willingness to volunteer for any task enabled them to collectively meet a tight deadline. These types of celebratory rituals in the workplace are known to reinforce the behaviours we want. They reinforce people's focus on what works best and create or support a genuine sense of belonging. Celebratory rituals remind our brains what behaviours are required or desired, which increases their likelihood of becoming habitual. Habitual behaviours drive culture and ensure that desirable behaviours occur across the organisation, even when we are distracted or preoccupied with other things. Rituals help people to feel more deeply involved in their daily jobs as they highlight the deeper symbolism of day-to-day tasks, which in turn heightens a task's perceived value.

Rituals are of course literally an enriching experience, so perhaps we shouldn't be that surprised by the researchers' findings. Every human culture on the planet engages in rituals as a means of celebrating not only what has been achieved but also, and more importantly, who they are and who they have become. Birthdays are a common example of this or perhaps a farewell ceremony for a colleague leaving your organisation.

So that brings us to the end of the five steps people within an organisation can initiate to build real momentum to creating a culture worth contributing to. Take ownership of the culture, decide to create the culture above the line, communicate what the culture will look like and what progress is being made or needs further work and finally celebrating the success of your culture worth contributing to.

In the bigger picture, you will recall that a culture worth contributing to is one of three cultural buoyancy devices—along with making the work worth doing and having leaders worth following—that will support your organisation to create an above the line culture.

So you have now completed most of the required parts to create an above the line culture. However, there is one final process I want to share with you that will pull all the parts of not only the recommendations outlined in this book but also the many aspects of maintaining and developing your culture that you no doubt already have in place within your organisation's processes. The process I am referring to is what I call developing a culture plan.

Just as your organisation would develop a business plan or a marketing plan, I encourage you to also develop a culture plan. This simple culture plan structure outlined in the remaining chapters of this book is an ideal format to gather and track all the disparate activities and initiatives that will collectively contribute towards lifting the culture above the line. In the final section of this book I will outline how a culture plan works, how to use its six components and where the plan fits into the overarching above the line culture model.

Part IV

CULTURE PLANNING

EXCELLING

SUCCESSFUL

STABLE

DYING

DEAD

CHAPTER 17

Preparing to plan

In this final part of the discussion of the above the line process, I will introduce you to culture planning. Along with the three cultural buoyancy devices of leaders worth following, work worth doing and cultures worth contributing to, culture planning is a powerful support process designed to help advance your organisation's culture. A culture plan does not replace the three cultural buoyancy devices, but rather complements them, and they should be designed and delivered simultaneously.

The various approaches that you select to implement from the three cultural buoyancy devices should be noted and monitored in the culture plan. For example if your organisation decided to implement a merit badge system, this would be catalogued as a single project in the culture plan. Likewise, any leadership development program or decision to brief employees on their ownership of the culture should be documented in the plan. This enables a more formal review and discussion to be held in the future to determine what you set out to achieve with your culture plan and what you actually achieved with your culture plan, which could be significantly different from what you set out to achieve, and what actually happened as a result of implementing the plan.

Let's have a closer look at the culture plan concept.

Culture plan concept

I'm sure your organisation has a business plan or strategic plan, and it probably has a marketing plan and maybe a safety plan. A culture plan involves a similar process. Where a marketing plan is a deliberately designed approach to increase customers' recognition and connection to your brand, a culture plan is designed to have the same effect for increasing the people in your business's understanding of and engagement with your culture. A culture plan also enables leaders to determine what specific steps to take to support the raising of the culture to the next level above. A culture plan is based upon six aspects of culture that are found in every culture in the world. Please note though that they are not the same as the six levels we have already discussed. They are not dead, dying, disabled, stable, succeeding and excelling as these are levels that a culture can rise or sink to. The six aspects of the culture plan we are about to explore are to be found in any culture regardless of at which level they currently sit. The following six chapters outline the six aspects of the culture plan.

The original thinking and design behind this culture plan evolved first from anthropologist Gregory Bateson's work, particularly the ideas captured in his book *Steps to an Ecology of Mind*, which concerned various logical levels of thinking. Gregory Bateson identified a series of interdependent yet differing neurological systems of learning and ordered them into six levels. The levels, he suggested, should be thought of as having a hierarchical relationship to one another, with the higher levels having a greater influence over those below them. Bateson noted that any changes made using the lower levels of his model were not always permanent and did not necessarily influence the higher levels, whereas changes made at the higher levels of the model were likely to be long lasting and to influence all levels below. Bateson calls these separate parts levels, but I will refer to them as six aspects of the culture plan so as not confuse them with the levels above and below the line that we have already explored.

Bateson's ideas on this topic were developed further by Robert Dilts, master trainer in neurolinguistic programming. He created a model suggesting distinctive logical levels that could be understood and influenced to enhance the degree of alignment for an individual person to become increasingly congruent in their words and behaviours. The model can also be used to align the various components of a system, even a social system system. Dilts extended Bateson's original model by adding an additional level above the level of identity, which he called 'spiritual' because it refers to an intangible influence that enables you to perform at a higher level. In business and in the culture plan we don't use the word as spiritual means too many different things to different people. In business and the culture plan we call this level 'purpose.' Unlike Dilts, in the culture plan we do not call the six components of the culture 'levels' but aspects. The reason for this is that I found that doing so encouraged many businesspeople to inadvertently refer to a level as being somehow superior to the levels below. In culture and culture planning this is not the case. Each component is equally important.

Back in 2004 I wrote a book called *Leading Through Values* and asked Dilts's permission to use his initial model to fit an educational model for enhancing organisational culture. Dilts generously granted me permission and since that time I have been working with the model as a simple and effective means for educating organisations on how to work through the process of aligning a culture to higher aspects of performance and an organisation's strategy. These aspects of a culture plan combine to give a culture its shape, feeling, rhythm, momentum, and sense of self and sense of other. In hierarchical order the aspects of the culture plan are:

- purpose
- identity
- values and beliefs
- capability
- behaviour
- environment.

By considering the role and influence of each of these six aspects in your culture, you will immediately move far beyond the common limitations that organisations set for themselves in seeing and understanding culture. Understanding the six aspects enhances our ability to think about, understand and define a culture and inspire people to support either the maintenance of the culture or to lift it to the next level above the line. So let's get started with the first aspect of culture: purpose.

CHAPTER 18

Culture plan 1: purpose

The purpose aspect of culture answers the question of 'what for?' in a culture, defining the reason an organisation exists.

A purpose, as we read earlier when reviewing the work of business consultant and author Jim Stengel and his book *Grow: How Ideals Power Growth and Profit at the World's 50 Greatest Companies*, should be focused on improving the lives of others. A purpose statement defines who is to be served by the culture. In a culture plan, we use the purpose aspect to define our primary customer value proposition (price, service or products) and weave this into a purpose statement that outlines the organisation's purpose for offering this to customers. Ideally, the entire shape of your culture will follow from defining its purpose. A clear purpose isn't just about customer delight: it can help employee fulfilment too.

It used to be that where you came from defined who you were — your country, state or town spoke volumes about your identity. Whether you were from the United States, Japan, England, Germany, Argentina, Kenya or Australia, the place told much about your story. Today what distinguishes each of us more than where we were born is what we believe in and our sense of purpose. Purpose has replaced place as the key distinguishing indicator of identity. This means people want to be able to share with others the purpose of their work, as it helps define who they are to others.

It pays to have a culture that enables the purpose conversation to take place, and take place with pride. Conversations about the purpose are powerful reminders of the meaning of our work. Purpose conversations are motivational, they help lift our minds and spirits out of the day-to-day grind of the details and specifics of each working day. Most employees I have spoken to don't overly care who makes money from the business. Many claim to have never met a shareholder unless the shareholder also happens to also be an employee of the organisation, so it is difficult for them to feel good or fulfilled by shareholders they have never met benefiting from their daily labour, courage and creativity. Employees do connect with customers — often daily. When a purpose statement defines how customers will benefit from the culture's output employees often connect with and get to know individual customers so the purpose feels more real and connected to people they have actually met and know. So a purpose statement designed to serve customers works in a far more powerful way than one that focuses on shareholders' wealth. A purpose statement that actually means something in real terms works in a powerful manner to align and inspire employees' efforts to service customers.

CHAPTER 19
Culture plan 2: identity

Identity addresses the questions of who the people within a culture see themselves as, and what they want to be known for. A sense of identity can be a powerful determinant for a culture. You need only ask someone at a social gathering or sporting event where they work and you can tell almost immediately whether they are working in an above the line or below the line culture just by watching their body language and listening to their tone of voice when they name the organisation they work for.

This is an interesting point for several reasons. First, because the company name alone can come to mean something powerful and positive to individuals, or it can mean the opposite. Just thinking about where they work can trigger people into behaviours and attitudes that are above or below the line. Obviously above the line responses are preferable for everyone. The second consideration is the impact the identity of your organisation has on the employees. A negative response to your company identity can do significant damage to your organisation's reputation. Given the social media explosion around the world, employees are not afraid to go public with how disgruntled they are with the difference between what the company promises or stands for in the market (its projected identity) and what it is really like inside (the real identity). These types of public exposure are accelerated when customers hear of them and then spread them through customer word of mouth.

The identity of your company has a role to play when employees announce in a social setting where they work to other people. The declaration of the company identity involves an element of status. Providing your people with a chance to feel good about where they work in their own social networks empowers them to work effectively and with pride in their workplace culture to maintain that status.

On a more technical point, the identity of your culture should be created from the embodying of the operating models discussed earlier. We discussed the three strategic options a business works with and suggested that one of them should be considered as the lead strategy. You will recall that I used a tricycle as the metaphor for the three wheels of strategy: operationally excellent, customer intimate, product leaders, one of which is selected as the lead wheel.

The identity aspect of the culture plan should capture and communicate the chosen lead wheel for the culture. For example, you might build an identity for your culture around being a customer-friendly or customer-focused culture if your lead strategic wheel is customer intimacy.

You should also consider how to represent the chosen operating model as a diagram, symbol or formula to communicate it with ease across the organisation's culture. For example, you might choose to use the tricycle metaphor described earlier in the book to establish the central identity of the company culture—the front wheel—while the two back wheels support this identity. The identity once agreed upon should be written up as a formal cultural tenet. For example, a customer intimacy culture might develop an identity and brand that has an identity built around the promise 'a culture committed to customer delight'. An operational excellence identity might describe itself as 'a culture dedicated to quality and efficiency'. Finally a product leading identity might create an identity along the lines of 'a culture providing creative solutions'. Inviting your marketing team or brand consultants to support this work with an internal brand strategy can ensure the identity is understood and embraced throughout the organisation. As we shall see throughout the following chapter, other aspects of the culture plan will then be designed to add further support and alignment to the process.

Such identity statements should be used as a guiding process for all behaviour in the organisation: people should, no matter what their role is, be encouraged to behave in a manner that supports the delivery of the culture's identity. If the culture's identity is operational excellence and is described, for example, as 'thrift', then everyone should be considering ways in which they can behave in their individual role that contribute to saving money. Alternatively, if the identity is product leadership, employees might consider how in their role they can contribute to supporting or creating new product ideas or refinements of existing products. If the identity is to embody customer intimacy, then obviously employees would consider how, within their role, they can contribute to or improve the customer's experience.

Anybody working in a role or department that is not directly related to the front wheel and the culture's identity can explore how they can indirectly contribute to the central identity or front wheel.

All cultures have areas in which people work in ways that are not directly related to customer contact areas, and yet, just like the back wheels on a tricycle, without their presence nothing else would work. So although they are not always in the spotlight of company performance measurements, they should always be acknowledged as contributing to the greater whole of the company culture.

Remember, once you have finalised establishing your culture's identity, based upon selecting the identity, you should communicate it across the organisation and position it as a rallying call for everyone to rise above the line and align all their efforts to delivering or supporting the delivery of the identity, so that, in turn, they can deliver on the culture's purpose statement.

Let's now move on to the third aspect in the culture plan: values.

CHAPTER 20

Culture plan 3: values

Organisational values in the way many companies do them are neither organised nor values. An organisation's values should be created to inspire the people in the culture to act, think and behave in ways that enable the company culture to operate above the line. The values are not there to make the leadership team feel better about themselves, if they came up with the values on an executive retreat. Nor are they for the board to simply tick the box of their governance 'to do' list.

The trick to getting company values right is to understand what values are and to use their power effectively. We touched on values earlier in this book when we explored the concept of values falling into three sets of controlling, relating and developing values that supported the operating models. An organisation's values should be composed of the values that support the operating model. They needn't all be from the one set of values, as some of the values that would fall into a category that is not directly aligned with the operating model may still enable some aspect of behaviour or performance to be linked to delivering on the customer value proposition. For example, if the culture purpose is to deliver delightful service, and the operating model and identity are therefore selected and worded as things that reflect and embody customer intimacy, then some of the values should be drawn from the relational set of values to reflect this priority. However, a value of, say, 'quality' from the control set of values could be supportive, as would the value of 'creativity' from the development set of values. Just choose values that actually enhance the culture, rather than choosing them because they sound nice or make you feel good about yourselves. Values must be functional, motivational and meaningful in order for them to work.

To better understand how to get the company values to work, let's look at values in a little more detail.

The nature of values

You will recall that a value is a human preference that has been energised and activated according to the priority that the people give that value. For example, if the preference is to experience profit, the priority employees place on generating profit determines the value of profit within the organisation. A value that carries zero or low priority with people will rarely be transformed into aligned behaviour.

It is important to get company values right. When organisations don't, they often end up violating the values they are trying to instil into the company. When people share a set of values, they build a lexicon, or language, around those values. Values build language and language is the lifeblood of culture. Cultures that value trust, sharing and listening are likely to regularly use the words 'trust', 'sharing' and 'listening', or words with similar meaning. People in the culture also have many stories to tell that describe and demonstrate how trust, sharing and listening occur and are practised within the company culture.

You can always tell if an organisation's official values are genuine by the number of stories told within the organisation about those values. If an organisation truly practises the values of integrity or customer service, then the company will be full of stories about how, when and to whom these two values were delivered and experienced. Far too many organisations pretend to hold true to their values, but don't have any true stories to demonstrate their practice. Your people will know they are living your company values when they have stories to tell, or, better yet, when they are in the stories being told!

Values and coaching

A useful way to help keep the values relevant and alive is to encourage your managers to use the organisation's values as a powerful and quick framework for coaching desired behaviours. Many years ago, I had the privilege of working with the world-famous Burger King restaurants. I helped facilitate the creation of three values for their culture to be used as an inspiration for desirable behaviour, and we also helped staff embrace a working collective identity. The staff mostly consisted of teenagers working part time. As a parent of teenagers, I know how difficult it can be just to have them keep their bedrooms tidy, let alone manage a business environment as complex and fast-paced as a busy restaurant. The three values the company worked with were pride, passion and performance. We coached all the managers to provide on-the-job performance feedback based around these values in order to address and support staff behaviour. For example, when a customer had accidentally spilled some of the ingredients of their Whopper burger and the staff had not responded quickly enough to cleaning up, the manager would train using values-based coaching. It sounds like this: 'Tim, as you know, pride is one of the values our culture is trying to uphold at all times. When you walk past the food on the floor, it shows that we as a culture lack pride in our store's appearance. I know you're busy, but we need to prioritise our values over *all other tasks. Does that make sense?'* The manager's words speak as much about collective commitment and the central position of the value in the culture as they do about Tim's oversight. Whenever I checked how the staff felt about the values-based coaching approach, we always got positive feedback. The staff commented that this style of correction was great because it wasn't about them personally, but instead was about living the values that they had previously and collectively accepted and agreed to live by.

One final point to do with your culture's values. I tend to recommend having only three values. You do not have to follow this suggestion, but allow me to explain my reasoning. I tend to favour restricting your selection to three values because:

- If you have more than three values people struggle to remember them.

- You are forced to get really authentic rather than cover all your options with a wide-cast net of multiple values.

- Restricting yourselves to three values makes you work harder on ensuring the definitions of each of the values really means something useful, aligned and important for your culture.

- As in so many things in life, less is more.

- If you have any more than three values, it often starts to become a little self-indulgent. Not always, but often enough for me to have noticed.

So that concludes our consideration of the role of values in the culture planning process. Our next step is to understand culturing capability.

CHAPTER 21

Culture plan 4: capability

The capability aspect of culture relates to understanding what skills people will require to build and maintain the culture or lift it to the next level in the above the line model. It can be useful to think of the level your culture is currently at and what is required to build your cultural capability. Specifically, cultural capability might include some or all of the following skills, abilities or resources:

- training and development leaders to communicate for culture or even just lead the culture

- deliberately ritualising culture

- using professional story telling

- improving managers' awareness of their departmental culture

- improving recruitment and induction processes

- developing thought leadership

- removing the silo mentality

- mentoring one another

- providing on-the-job coaching

- enhancing collaboration across department boundaries.

A number of years ago I had the opportunity to support an organisation that wanted to encourage its people to adopt more positive, collaborative behaviours. To achieve this, they did not conduct extensive retraining or expensive road shows. They simply equipped all

150 leaders and managers in the culture with a number of small green flags and lapel badges in the shape of a small green flag. Every time staff exhibited encouraged behaviours, green flags would be waved or lapel badges handed out with words of praise. In no time at all, the culturing behaviours had shifted dramatically. This age-old practice of recognising and rewarding behaviours we want to see more of is time tested and effective, yet repeatedly managers and leaders do not take the time or have the awareness to use them. Recognition works because all behaviour is a derivative of the identity someone is in at the time of the behaviour. This simply means that all our behaviour is a result of the sense of self we have at the time the behaviour is acted out. So when we see people acting in a way that serves the culture, the simple step of recognising who a person was 'being' (such as serving, understanding, supporting) when they acted the way they did reinforces the likelihood of the person deliberately choosing to adopt that identity again.

Questions to determine what your culture may require to develop capability are:

- What do we need to do to attract, retain, inspire and focus good people?

- How can we build our tribal identity and embody our values?

- What resources are necessary to achieve our desired culture?

- What leadership skills are required to lead a culture? Do we have them?

- Are we prepared for the future? Do we understand the benefits of thought leadership as a competitive advantage?

The various capabilities a culture needs to progress are nearly always unique to that particular culture. So be prepared to take some time together in your organisation to investigate your answers to the questions listed above.

Once you have discussed what capabilities need to be developed to support your culture to raise its level and you have included these ideas and identified how to execute these ideas, you should include these in your culture plan.

So we have discussed culturing capability. Next on our list in developing our culture plan is behaviour.

CHAPTER 22
Culture plan 5: behaviour

Organisations often consider the behaviour aspect of a culture plan to be the most important, as understandably they assume that this is the aspect of culture where things get done! This is true, but without question all the aspects we have considered so far and the aspect of environment all have a huge impact on people's behaviour. So, when creating a culture plan, despite the temptation to do a large volume of thinking and planning here, my recommendation is to keep it simple. Really simple in fact: this chapter is one of the shortest in the book, as desirable behaviours are simple to clarify for a culture when you have already determined the purpose, identity and values of the culture.

In my opinion some organisations get overly and unnecessarily detailed when it comes to identifying and cataloging the specific behaviours they want to see in the organisation. Think about it. This means they need to catalogue literally thousands of individual behaviours in order to inform people of what to do, and no doubt to measure whether they are actually doing it. Unfortunately many staff I have spoken to over the years who work in cultures where people are required to break their daily performance down into such minute behavioural details feel quite patronised by the process. The only time this approach to behaviours is actually appreciated is during the staff induction phase, when they are new to a role or the organisation. In that case, they are delighted to ensure they are aware and competent at delivering on all the expected behaviours, as the detail enables them to feel as if they are learning to fit in.

The behaviour aspect of culture pays attention to how people actually behave in relation to how they could or should behave. This aspect of culture is the place where you should pay attention to what is included or excluded from a job description compared to the way in which the job is performed on a daily basis. The simplest way to factor in the behaviours you want to encourage most in your organisation's culture is to consider what people are rewarded and recognised for. By understanding the rewards and recognition that influence people's behaviours, you can support them to change certain behaviours where necessary to align the behaviours to the desired culture. The simplest way to plan for and inspire people to identify the desired behaviours in a culture is to spend some time observing behaviours in your organisation and then consider which of these you want to continue, which you want to stop and which you want to start. I often describe these three requirements for a culture's behavioural traits as being like a set of traffic lights.

- The green light represents any of the behaviours we want to start in the culture.

- The amber light represents those behaviours that are already present in the culture that we want to maintain and continue to see.

- The red light of course represents behaviours we want to stop.

This simple metaphor of a traffic light can be useful in culture planning in a number of ways:

- within the culture, plan to determine the three categories of key behaviours to work with and support

- plan for and enable work groups to facilitate their own discussions regarding the three groups of behaviours, and then build action plans to implement their embodiment into the culture

- plan for one group or department to provide feedback to other groups about the behaviours they find, or would find, helpful (or not) when the two groups or departments interact.

Always remember that once people are past their induction phase and as long as the culture is already above the line, to keep the emphasis on behaviours short and simple, and encourage employees to be directly involved in the implementation. If your culture is below the line, you will need to spend more time, effort and deliberation around appropriate behaviours, so do not be afraid of addressing these. Your very culture may depend on it!

So that's the behavioural aspect of culture covered. We shall now move on to the final aspect of the culture plan, which is environment.

CHAPTER 23

Culture plan 6: environment

The first thing you will notice about this chapter on the environment aspect of culture is that it considers and covers more variables than the previous aspects. Why is this? Because in a culture there are always more elements and forces at work than are going on within the culture. In simple terms, if we think of Australia and its culture, the various aspects of Australian culture are complex rich and varied. Yet as rich and as complex as the culture is, there are more variables outside the social or national scope of Australian culture. That can include, for example, the rest of the world's nations; the planet and its resources for another; and the entire universe both known and unknown. All these external factors take longer to consider and understand than the internal aspects of the culture.

The environment of culture takes into consideration *where* the culture takes place and what impact the environment has on it, or what impact the culture will have on the environment. This aspect takes into consideration where people carry out their jobs, with whom the role interfaces (the context) and the constraints faced by the people in the environments they work in (constraints).

The environment includes things both outside the organisation itself, such as the market, government policy pertaining to the industry, international exchange rates, weather, labour and talent pools and international relations. It can also include the context internally within the organisation, and refer to such things as the stage of growth the organisation has reached, or if there has been a change in leadership, or a merger or acquisition, or perhaps a restructuring of the organisation.

Looking at your organisation

Working out the constraints faced within a culture plan might include listing all the things that make it difficult for the culture to thrive, such as competition, leadership change, a silo mentality, finance and resources restrictions, and staff engagement. To really get to grips with the factors involved with the environment aspect of your culture it may even pay to become an amateur anthropologist for a few weeks, or even months, before you start so that you can get a lay of the land as it currently is in your culture. Try taking a walk through your business branch, factory or office, just like you have done a hundred times before. Only this time look at the environment as if you were an anthropologist. This means looking and listening for meaning. Look for and listen to evidence of what it means to work there. Take a small pocket-sized notebook and note everything you can that captures the meaning of 'work'. Take note of anything that appears to stand in the way of your tribe thriving. After you have done this, wait a few days and do it again. Afterwards, contemplate what your culture is telling you about what it means to work there. Think about what key messages the culture shares with you. What's working? What clearly isn't? Think about how this might contribute to or contradict your workplace reputation in the marketplace. Invite project teams to think about how their projects contribute to or potentially sabotage various aspects of the company culture.

With your observations and cultural planning, be aware that sometimes what is observed and initially considered a constraint by the organisation can be shown, through monitoring and exploration as part of the culture plan, to be something quite different. For example, some organisations consider the advent of social media and staff usage of it as a constraint on their culture. Yet investigation as part of your culture plan may reveal significant advantages that can be gained from embracing social media as part of your culture's communication process. Let me tell you about one such case.

Last year I heard renowned speaker Don Peppers, founder partner of Peppers & Rogers Group business consultants, speak at a conference for chief information officers. Don told the story of a hotel booking company that clamped down heavily on staff accessing social network sites during work hours. The more conservative leadership team deemed such use of company time to be unacceptable and unprofessional. The results were astonishing. The bookings for the hotel plummeted, as it turned out the staff had been promoting the hotel bookings through their own personal social networking sites and answering people's questions concerning the value and even the validity of some of the special deals on offer. When they stopped activity on their own social networks, sales dropped immediately. Don also said that social media now provided the opportunity for any member of your culture to become a PR representative of your company, capable, if briefed and trained, of heading off bad publicity almost as quickly as the adverse comments in the market gained momentum.

Because of the speed of introduction of new technology, from phones to electronic tablets to BlackBerries and the wide variety of social media platforms, such as Twitter, Facebook and LinkedIn, it would be wise not to dismiss their value without further investigation. Alternatively, you may find that the reason people are so desperate to gain a gathering and social experience online is because the real live version available in your actual workplace culture is lacking in warmth, the sharing of information or has become isolated through silo mentalities or breakdowns in communication.

A number of my clients have embraced online social networks, such as Ning sites, with access restricted to employees, suppliers and customers, and with clear restrictions on the type of personal and business information that may be placed on the sites. They have proved to a wonderful way of enabling people to have a finger on the pulse of the business's needs, through their role as a gathering point for discussion group problem solving, and customer question and answer discussions about products and service advice. Other companies have used social media very successfully as a talent recruitment strategy. It is well worth discussing and understanding how social media can be integrated to advance your business culture and relationships.

More aspects to consider

Other aspects of the environment worth considering and investigating for their impact on the culture are changing work trends in society, such as the following:

- *People working remotely and/or from home.* Jason Fried, CEO of Basecamp online database systems, and David Heinemeier Hansson, programmer and partner of Basecamp, argue in their book *Remote: Office Not Required* that there are some compelling reasons why organisations could increasingly allow their employees to work remotely. They suggest that, in many cases, employees working remotely allows the most talented people to produce their best work regardless of their location. I can vouch for the concept working for employees or people who are self-starters and need minimal supervision. If the employees are very talented and experienced, sometimes working remotely enables them to be more productive, as they can free themselves from some of the more mundane and disruptive limitations of the workplace.

- *Generational and other cultural generational shifts.* Dozens of books point out the generational gaps in our modern workplaces, each generation with their own needs and wants. Although it is certainly worthwhile understanding some of the potential trends here, my recommendation is not to get too carried away with generational concepts and theories. Too often the ideas about Generation X and Y should more accurately be called Generalisations about X and Y. It pays to remember people are all unique and their personal values and levels of consciousness are likely to have more influence on their motivations and behaviours than what year they were born.

- *Customer expectations.* In the introduction to this book, I discussed how customers are shifting from wanting efficiency from your business to demanding better service. We have already discussed this, but a quick reminder at this point could be useful to see how customer expectations fit into the culture planning process. The expectation of and demand for efficiency from organisations by their customers is nothing compared with the longing for creativity and empathy the customers want. So, although customer expectations are part of the environment part of your culture plan, you may also need to consider what this means in your organisation for the capability aspect, too. For example what could be done to increase your employees' creativity and empathy?

- *Use of new technology.* This is an area that is already an important factor worth considering in relation to the impact technology has on your culture. Does it, for instance, lead to greater productivity but less socialisation? Or even the other way around? Does this matter? Is your technology so out of date it's actually slowing down the culture?

- *Greater and improved gender equality.* There is still an under-representation of the number of women in many organisations' leadership teams. Is this a factor in your culture? If so, what are the consequences? Is this something that could be improved through developments in your organisation's culture plan?

- *Misfits.* Being part of a culture is a voluntary process—people can volunteer to be part of the culture or volunteer not to be. Even if you set about weaving a culture, there will be people who just don't want to know, who want to stay with the tried and tested 'old way' of doing things. Do your best to invite them to contribute into the culture and, if that fails, let them go. As harsh as this may sound, if people who don't want to participate in the culture stay with your tribe, they will become increasingly unsettled, disruptive or alienated by the growing strength of the culture. For their sake and yours, they would be better off moving on to find a better fit with a culture they do want to be part of.

- *Future employees and your employment brand proposition.* Attractive workplace cultures are like a campfire burning bright on a dark, cold night for talented and inspired people. The opportunity to be part of a culture of high standing and regard is more often than not worth as much as a good salary. A good salary in a bad cultural experience is a bribe; a good salary in a culture worth belonging to doubles the value of the salary. When a company has a strongly defined and desirable workplace culture it becomes famous. It develops a powerful employment brand. People join a company for the organisation's journey and story, and the opportunity to contribute to both, as much as they join for a pay cheque. So what is your unique story? Position your company in the employment market so people want to be part of it. What is it your culture should be world famous for? Not your products or your brand: your culture!

- *Leadership.* Investigate and consider what would make your leaders worth following (see chapter 14 for more on this). How could your leaders become better at inspiring and leading the culture?

- *The board.* Use the culture plan to keep your board up to date with the progress and status quo of your culture. Since the collapse of Enron, you will find most boards take far more interest in the quality of the organisation's culture than ever before. Think about how the board's recommendations to your organisation might influence the culture, or even require the culture to change.

- *Customers.* Pay attention to customer feedback. Look to see which aspects of both the positive and negative aspects of your customer feedback are related to your culture. You can then begin to plan to maintain and even improve what is working and correct or eradicate what is not.

- *Suppliers.* Your suppliers are an important part of your organisation and, therefore, just like your customers, are worthwhile listening to and getting feedback from. Just like customer feedback, consider what to maintain within the culture that supports your suppliers to do a better job at servicing your organisation and what doesn't, so you know what to correct or eradicate.

- *Investors.* Although investors won't refer to your culture as being above or below the line, they will know if the culture is in trouble due to key symptoms, such as high staff turnover, a rise in customer complaints, loss of good leaders and an inability to attract key talent.

- *Society.* Society as a whole doesn't take kindly to organisations that are up to no good. Everything from big oil companies and those that dump toxic waste, to the churches and welfare organisations committing child abuse. Society can and does challenge an organisation's very place.

With the explanation of the sixth aspect of culture, we have reached the end of the review of the culture planning components. All six of the aspects occur and can be planned for at each level of the above and below the line cultures, apart from the dead cultures, of course, as they no longer exist. I highly recommend building a culture plan to assist you in your endeavours to raise the culture in your organisation.

I have seen the culture planning process work wonders in organisations across many different sectors, and I encourage you to take the time and the effort to complete one for the appropriate level of the above the line culture model, to support you to maintain that level or, if your have higher aims, to climb a level. Be aware that culture plans require input from many people from across the business, as well as constant review and sharing with all employees. This much activity and commitment requires full buy-in from your senior leaders, so make sure they are fully briefed on the business case for doing so.

CHAPTER 24

Culture plan example

Table 24.1 (overleaf) provides an outline of the culture plan developed for an imaginary company.

All six aspects of the culture are identified in the left-hand column.

The middle column of the table outlines either the position the company has chosen to take for each of these aspects, or the specific projects the company has committed to launch in order to support the culture to grow and align with the business strategy.

The right-hand column highlights the question that is answered for the culture by considering this aspect of a culture. For example, for the purpose aspect of the culture plan, you can see that the question answered is: 'Why does this culture exist?' The identity aspect of the culture has the question: 'What do we want to be famous for — price, product or service?' In highlighting the specific questions that are answered by considering each aspect of the culture, you can begin to see how the plan addresses all the questions your culture might raise.

Table 24.1: example culture plan summary page

Aspect	Culture's choices	Question answered
Purpose	To serve our customers to make their lives better.	Why are we here?
Identity	We will be famous for customer intimacy	Who are we? What do we want to be famous for?
Values	service, empathy, creative solutions	What motivates our culture?
Capability	1. Develop leadership communication skills. By November Project leader Sue Smith. 2. Ritualise our culture. By June Project leader Mark Richards. 3. Develop thought leadership. By 2016 Project leader Alison Taylor.	What do we need to be capable of in this culture?
Behaviour	Clarify with all employees which behaviours they consider above and below the line. Communicate to everyone the finalised correlated list of behaviours. Invite everyone to to take ownership and provide feedback to align behaviours with the list.	Which behaviours are above or below the line?
Environment	Develop a more attractive employee value proposition by December. Project leader George Harrison. Exploring opportunities for working remotely by July. Project leader Rebecca Mzarkia. Conduct customer delight survey within the next 90 days. Project leader Jenny Chiswick.	Where and when are events occurring that affect our culture?

Culture plan summary

Table 24.1 is a high-level overview of the culture plan. You should elaborate on each aspect shown in this table using additional pages of information to create a more complete report of your culture plan. For example, for each aspect you might provide more in-depth information to identify what action is being taken, what budget is required, who is head of this project and what time frames you are working to. For example, the capability aspect of the table could be elaborated on and look something like this:

Elaborated culture capability

Projects

- Engage all employees in a review of the company culture's above and below the line characteristics:

  - Time frame: over the next 90 days.

  - Budget required: zero.

  - Project leader: Sarah Jackson, operations manager.

- Ask each leader to read their copy of the book *Above the Line* to understand the consequences for their department's contribution to the overarching company culture:

  - Time frame: over the next 90 days.

  - Budget required: $200.

  - Project leader: Keith Monroe, human resources support manager.

- Explore the opportunity of initiating a merit badge system for our key skill requirements:

  - Time frame: over the next 120 days.

  - Budget required: unknown at this stage.

  - Project leader: Rebecca Green, national training manager.

- Develop our thought leadership capability.
  - Time frame: over the next year.
  - Budget required: unknown at this stage.
  - Project leader: Mary Harrison, national marketing manager.

Culture planning in practice

As an example of a culture plan being put into practice, let me share with you an example of how my client High Performance Sport New Zealand developed, completed and initiated their culture plan. Their aim was to help the organisation continue to do an outstanding job supporting sports and coaches from all sorts of codes to develop their elite athletes to represent New Zealand at the Rio Olympics in 2016 and beyond. The approach and commitment of High Performance Sport New Zealand to their culture plan was exemplary, as we might expect from high performance professionals.

An internal Culture Team was established and led by the passionate Susan Thomason (Lead Performance Life and Psychology) and Chris Morrison (High Performance Leader Capability). Chief Executive Alex Baumann immediately saw the potential of the process, and to this day continues to champion the ongoing work of the culture plan's development. Work on the culture planning process commenced, starting with the top three aspects of purpose, identity and values. The purpose, identity and values that had been identified were developed with a large percentage of the organisation's employees. Feedback was gathered and used for refining the purpose, identity and values. Monthly review sessions were held by the Culture Team, and an additional monthly review was held with me as their external adviser. Following this a workshop day was organised to include leaders from all key departments around the nation to refine the capability aspects of the plan. Once that was achieved, the Culture Team refined the final three aspects of the plan. The final written culture plan was drawn up, designed, laid out and printed. A final launch event, involving all available employees and run in an interactive and creative manner, was held. It involved each department sharing how they were going to contribute to keeping the plan alive and activated in the organisation. Six-monthly reviews by cross-departmental discussion groups were to follow up by reviewing any strong signs of trust that had developed across the culture, along with clear signs that the culture's values were shared. These two areas of trust and values are key to the ongoing social capacity of the culture. Any areas of concern were raised, recorded and referred to the culture plan team to consider and recommend resolutions.

The culture plan will be reviewed regularly as the organisation progresses towards the Rio Olympics. In particular, I have encouraged the culture planning team to consider three important questions as part of continuing review process:

- What did you set out to achieve with your culture plan?

- What did you actually achieve with your culture plan (which could of course be significantly different than what you set out to achieve)?

- What actually happened as a result of implementing the culture plan?

As a result of reviewing the culture plan using these three questions, important lessons and directions the culture has taken can be understood and explored. Sometimes the unplanned aspects of culture development prove to be more beneficial than was planned. And sometimes they don't. The trick is to be aware of the specific changes that are occurring so that realignment can be planned and implemented.

Although I have suggested that the culture planning group review the culture in this manner every six months, that is because the timing suits their cultural and strategic needs. In a faster moving corporate culture, I often advise the culture planning team to review the culture every 90 days. This may sound like a short period of time to be reviewing your culture, but I have found that in the commercial setting a culture can change quite dramatically within just one financial quarter. In developing a culture plan for your organisation, you should select a review schedule that suits your organisational strategic and cultural needs.

To finish our overview of culture planning, let me offer a few words of advice. First, although you may be about to start the culture plan, you should never consider it finished. Especially for the aspects of capability, behaviour and environment, there is sure to be ongoing development work required by your organisation just to keep abreast of the changing world and markets around you. Second, consider setting up a small team of no more than seven people to coordinate and oversee the culture plan. Any more than seven people, I have found, slows the whole process up unnecessarily. Finally, do not be put off by the few cynics or sceptics who may voice their dissent concerning working on culture. Simply lift your efforts and enthusiasm and place your emphasis on the majority's positive support. Believe me, most people will be positive, as most people want to be a part of culture worth contributing to. It is simply human nature.

CHAPTER 25

A final word of encouragement

Thank you for taking the time to read *Above the Line*. I mean it. I love writing books but only because I hold a deep desire that what I have to say may be of some value to someone, somewhere, some time. I hope that someone is you. I hope that somewhere is the organisations you play a role in. I hope that some time is now. I hope you have found the book inspiring enough to initiate activities and conversations in your organisation to raise the culture above the line.

To work on a culture, and especially one that to begin with is below the line, takes courage, because you are almost certain to meet with criticism and opposition along the way. Don't let that stop you, though, as you will need to keep your own spirits up to ensure you are not contributing in any way to making the culture worse.

As I said in the opening of this book: I believe organisations are one of the greatest resources available to humanity. In order for organisations to be able to contribute in a truly meaningful way we will need the people within those organisations to participate and contribute to a culture that is above the line.

I hope you and your colleagues will join me in my quest to raise the cultures in organisations whenever the opportunity presents itself for the privilege and ability to work and live compassionately with one another and our amazing planet.

I truly hope this book has served you in at least some way. Having finished the book now you may like to read through the following page to explore some of the ways you can stay in, or progress, the above the line conversation, and further develop your ability to facilitate the process in your organisation.

CHAPTER 26

Next steps

Join the above the line conversation at www.michaelhenderson.com.

To stay in and help progress the conversation about above the line cultures you could:

- sign up for my free newsletter, which is full of tips, ideas, observations and trends to pay attention to. Go to www.michaelhenderson.com and follow the prompts.

- sign up for one of my free above the line webinars to discuss various aspects of this book. Visit www.michaelhenderson.com.

- visit www.michaelhenderson.com to explore the various workshops available to run in your organisation to support your efforts to raise the culture above the line.

- register to book a complimentary 15-minute telephone consultation with me about your above the line approach.

- book me to speak at your next company event at www.michaelhenderson.com.

Bibliography

Bateson, Gregory 1972. *Steps to an ecology of mind. Collected Essays in Anthropology, Psychiatry, Evolution, and Epistemology*. University of Chicago Press, Chicago.

Dilts, Robert 1996. *Visionary Leadership Skills*. Meta Publications.

Fried, Jason, & Heinemeier Hansson, David 2013. *Remote. Office Not Required*. Vermilion, New York.

Hawkins, David R. 2002. *Power V Force*. Hay House, Carlsbad, California.

Henderson, Michael & Shar, & Thompson, Dougal 2004. *Leading Through Values*. HarperCollins.

McGilcrest, Ian 2009. *The Master and His Emissary. The Divided Brain and the Making of the Western World*. Yale University Press.

Page, Mark 2012. *Wired for Culture. The Natural History of Human Cooperation*. Allan Lane, London.

Index

Qual IT 180, 182–183, 184
quality in work 106, 129

reactive 76–77
reason and logic vs creativity and
    intuitiveness 135, 140–143, 149
reinforcement, cultural 119–120
Rene, Dave 162
resentment 106
resignations 105
resilience 135
respect for generations 150
restructuring 26
retention strategies 79
retrenchment 26
rewards and recognition 176,
    182–185, 214
rituals, role of 6, 7, 9, 10–11, 125,
    142–143, 183, 194, 195
rivalry, interdepartmental 106
rudeness 114
rumour, sense of 74–75

sabotage 104, 133
scouts and guides movement
    182–183
self-esteem 136, 149
self-reliance 135
service
    —commitment to 135
    —value proposition 40–41, 42,
        43, 52
    —willing 133, 135, 148
shared beliefs 10, 20
silo mentality 21, 70, 75, 82, 88, 98,
    106, 122, 213, 220
skill development 176, 182–185
social media 205, 220–222
society 225

solidarity 148
stable cultures 125–130
staff see also culture, ownership of
    —Gen Y 29–30
    —turnover 24, 77–79, 81, 98,
        105, 106, 225
    —understanding of culture 4, 6,
        14–15
strategy, business
    —aligned with culture 33–63,
        69–70, 78
    —aligned with values 46–54
    —company focus 39–45
    —effect of culture on 20–22
    —importance of values for
        62–63
    —operating model 41–45
    —relationship with culture
        33–36
    —values and understanding
        54–61
    —vs morals and ethics 58
stress 129, 135, 149
successful cultures 131–136
suppliers 224
supportiveness 129
sustainability 136
sympathy 129, 136, 150

taking 71–72
Tata group 81
teamwork 72, 76, 170, 230
technology, use of new 223 see also
    social media
TED talks 192–193
theft 72, 81
thought leadership 83, 86, 92–93,
    97, 98, 213, 214, 230
tolerance of difference 146–147, 148

BOOK A FREE 15-MINUTE PHONE CONVERSATION WITH AUTHOR

If you have enjoyed reading *Above the Line* and wish to engage in a complimentary 15-minute phone or Skype conversation with Michael, he would love to discuss the *Above the Line* approach and how it can be applied in your organisation. Email Michael's support team on info@michaelhenderson.com and they will confirm the appropriate booking.

Source: © Tom Roberton

There is no obligation to work with Michael, just the opportunity to explore any questions or queries you may have. We trust you will enjoy talking with him.

Check out Michael's other services at www.michaelhenderson.com

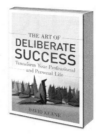

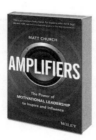